MW00587958

Stoney Point Bouldering
& Top Roping

Urban Rock: Stoney Point Bouldering & Top Roping

1st Edition ©1994
2nd Edition ©1997
3rd Edition ©2004

ISBN 0-9654448-1-3

Cover photograph: Tom Bristow on Yabo Arete - Michael Reardon
Title Page: Scott Nomi prepares for Kodas Corner
Copyright Page: Knuckles shredded on Standard Route, Eat Out More Often
Back cover photograph: Mike Newheart starts up Crowd Pleaser
All uncredited photographs ©2004 Chris Owen
Design, typesetting, and digital artwork by Chris Owen.

IMPORTANT LEGAL NOTICE and WARNING
Climbing is dangerous! Therefore, climb at your own risk. It is your responsibility to safeguard yourself, no responsibility is assumed by the author of this book for the personal safety of others. Route descriptions are no substitute for experience, it is your responsibility to teach yourself to climb safely.

Printed in Canada by:
Hignell Book Printing, Winnipeg, Manitoba
http://www.hignell.mb.ca

table of contents

Bob Kamps On Boulder 1 circa 1961 | Bob Kamps Collectio

This edition has been published in answer to the increasing popularity of bouldering. This increase is a natural progression; as first ascents become scarcer, climbers scan their eyes to the boulders they once besmirched. The dynamic nature of bouldering has attracted more young people to the sport. This is good.

n addition to providing route information, this book attempts to introduce climbers to the traditional ethics of top roping and bouldering at Stoney Point and to encourage all who climb to love and protect the rock, and respect the environment.

would like to thank the following people for their help and/or companionship during the creation of the 3rd edition: Chris Barker, Fred Batliner, Jonathan Bowman, Marc Burns, Marc Chrysanthou, Brian Chung, Paul Dusatko, Mike Flood, Rick Fredland, Stefan Harms, Bob and Bonnie Kamps, Chris Leger, Mike Martin, Liz Murray, Mike Newheart, Scott Nomi, Bryn Owen, Noreen Owen, Stephen Owen, Lluis Penalver-Aquila, Aaron Sandlow, Chris Savage, Sara Susca, Tony Tennessee, and Melody Wong.

A special thanks goes to Michael Reardon, for route descriptions (some of them are verbatim), providing beta, anecdotes, photographs and proof reading.

Additionally the following individuals/organizations are recognized for their contributions during cleanup activities; Charles Church, LA Recreation and Parks, REI Northridge, The Outland Mountain Shop, Friends of Stoney Point (FSOP), and Hope Worldwide.

Finally, this upgraded edition would not have been possible without consulting the following books; Stoney Point Guide - Hellweg & Fisher, Southern California Bouldering Guide - Fry, and Stone Crusade - Sherman.

dedicate this third printing to Bryn and Stephen.

Chris Owen
Big Bear Lake, 2013

Stoney Point

Hot Tuna V5 (Page 90)

introduction

In the spring of 1984 I parked my just purchased (from a Vegas dealer no less!) 1980 Dodge Omni on the northbound side of Topanga Canyon Boulevard and wandered down to Boulder 1. It was a Saturday afternoon and few people were there. The Boulder looked big, bigger than my grit boulders left behind in another world sundered by a veil of blue skies and a vast ocean. I climbed up the West Arete and down the East Face Route in my sneakers, and then I drove back to my shared studio apartment in Burbank. This was my introduction to Stoney Point. A place which would form such a pivotal role in my life; here I met the best of my friends, here I hit on my future wife and mother of my son, here I saw Yvon Chouinard and Bob Kamps climbing on Boulder 1, here I still come.

Here, then, is the place for the climbing residents of Los Angeles, California to get their rock fix. There are a lot of us. Some of us were born here and some of us came from elsewhere in search of sun and rock. There's an urban rock feel to the place. After a grid locked epic drive, you park on a boulevard of hurtling vehicles (expecting to be struck almost as soon as you step out of your car) and stumble down to the Front Boulders in frustration. On Boulder 1 you notice that every possible excrescence has chalk on it, going back to when they invented the stuff. A familiar face strolls from around the corner, you sit down on the bench and pull on your slippers ... another familiar face arrives ... two hours later, old friends wander down from the summit, spirits hungry for more but flesh spent and sore, talking bouldering smack, and in the hazy murk of the evening you arrive at the boulevard, say farewell to barely visible faces and step into your car. Resting chalked and tired hands on the steering wheel you think to yourself ... *'till next time.*

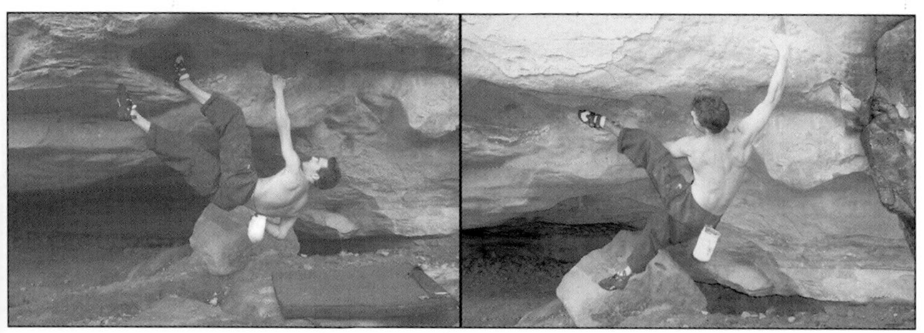

Climber: Paul Dusatko / Photos: integrity7.com

HISTORY

For thousands of years Stoney Point (or Castle Rock as it was called in the old days) served as a home to the local Native Americans - who had a village nearby and no doubt collected water in the natural cisterns, pounded acorns in the rock bowls (still to be seen today) and hunted animals with arrowheads traded from further north. They probably even bouldered.

The 1930's

Stoney Point was first noticed by climbers in about 1935. This was after Robert Underhill, a visiting East Coast climber with many first ascents under his belt paid a visit to California and educated the ignorant Sierra Club climbers in the fine art of rope management. Armed with new knowledge, the Sierra Club members, most notably, Glen Dawson (who with Underhill, Jules Eichorn and Norman Clyde went on a spree in the High Sierra and made the first ascent of the East Face of Whitney) went looking for things to rope up, they found Stoney Point tucked away in the northwest corner of the then distinctly rural San Fernando Valley. Sierra Club outings frequented Stoney Point from then onwards.

The 1950's

In the 50's a new breed of climber emerged, heavily influenced by the Sierra Club but bent upon new hard climbs. This was when bouldering really started at Stoney Point. Royal Robbins discovered the area in 1950 (at the age of 15) while riding a freight train. Soon Robbins, Yvon Chouinard, TM Herbert, Tom Frost and others were practicing aid routes in the bottoming cracks and trying all sorts of craziness on the surrounding boulders; no-hands ascents of the easier routes, climbing Boulder 1 while carry rocks (see Bill Dolt to the right) etc. All this paid off for Robbins with the first free ascent of *The Open Book* (5.9) at Tahquitz Rock in 1952 and subsequently huge first ascents in Yosemite (*Half Dome NW Face,* 1957 and *Salathe Wall,* El Capitan, 1961) followed by international celebrity. Robbins and Chouinard regularly hopped freight trains to Stoney Point, the trains slowing to climb over Santa Susana Pass provided an opportunity to hop off. Bob Kamps started somewhere around this time too, and was the quintessential Stoney regular, still working problems 40 years later! (Bob passed away in 2005, still climbing at the age of 73).

The 1970's

The next really big movement began in the early 1970's with the purist hard free climbing approach and contempt for any kind of aid. John Long (Largo) and his group (The Stonemasters) were major players out at Suicide and Tahquitz, and also frequented Stoney Point. John Bachar was also a child of this era, and, like a few climbers in other countries, started applying athletic training to improve his climbing. John started out at Stoney Point when in his early teens and a worthy legacy of his presence is the test piece *Ummagumma* (V7) in the Summit Boulders Area.

The 80's Onwards

By the early 1980's Stoney was established as a local bouldering venue, John Yablonski (Yabo), forced through his *Yabo Arete* (V8) and regulars included the burly Mike Waugh, sometimes on the scene as paramedic to aid injured climbers, other times as master of hardness. Interest migrated from the established areas with Bill Leventhal and Matt Oliphant doing a lot of exploring. Later on Paul Anderson, Jeff Johnson and the late Michael Reardon continued with this effort.

Things have been happening recently at Stoney Point, for example Jeff Johnson's *The Font* (V7), and Yair Kuperstein's *Fighting With Alligators* (V10). Now we sit in the midst of the bouldering renaissance, and I can't help but wonder who else will be a child of Stoney Point and, from here, move onto the world stage.

LOCATION

Stoney Point is located at the corner of Topanga Canyon Boulevard and the Ronald Reagan Freeway (118) in Chatsworth. Parking is available on the east side of Topanga Cyn Blvd. *Do not drive down the dirt road to the boulders.* Stoney Point is a city park and is closed between sunset and sunrise. See Map on Page 9.

TOP ROPING

Although it is possible to lead a few of the routes listed in this book, the generally accepted practice is to set up top ropes. Some of the routes follow pin scars, old aid routes by the masters prior to moving to Yosemite. A lot of the anchors require nut placements and long slings; therefore, be very familiar with anchoring techniques. Some of the routes have bolt anchors on top—always treat these with suspicion and never use just one bolt as an anchor.

Do not add sport climb bolts to the top rope routes here, they will be chopped.

Most climbers use chalk, as popular routes will attest; however, there are a lot of lesser-known routes that are clean. Try to keep them this way. On some routes it may be advisable for the belayer to wear a helmet—it's not uncommon for holds to fly.

TOP ROPING GEAR REQUIREMENTS

The following equipment will enable any climb to be top-roped:

- ✓ Two 50ft lengths of 1" webbing
- ✓ Two 20ft lengths of 1" webbing
- ✓ A small selection of sewn slings for fine tuning
- ✓ Five locking carabiners
- ✓ Hexentrics (#6 - #10)
- ✓ Set of Friends or equivalent
- ✓ Two 3/8" bolt hangers with nuts (3/8", 7/16" & 1/4" all UNC)

BOULDERING
Bouldering and Stoney Point are synonymous; one could almost say that it was invented here. The sandstone of Stoney Point has proven to be an ideal medium for bouldering, and has something for everyone—jugs, slopers, crimps, smears, hooks, squirming mantles, blank slabs, pin-scars, withering traverses, ridiculous lunges and even some occasional jamming. There's a good selection of boulder problems, with a lot of eliminates (deliberately avoiding big holds) and variations, all set in a convenient location, barely out of town. Hard climbers won't need this guide, they'll just wander at will and fire stuff, chalked holds or not. For those of us not so burly, it's always fun to check out the harder routes; just touch the starting holds and soak up some of the character and mystery they exude. Stoney is a great place to escape the rigors of the city, hang with the local LA bouldering gurus, and soak up the vibe.

RATINGS
Routes considered as top roped routes are rated using the Yosemite Decimal System (YDS), Class 5.0 being the easiest and the current upper limit somewhere around 5.15. The upper ratings are subdivided into four letter divisions: a, b, c and d; every effort has been made to add these to the number. However, if no consensus is available, + or - has been substituted. Because the routes are top-roped, no attempt has been made to rate the risk/protection factor. Owing to the weak nature of the rock the ratings listed in this book may change as holds disappear.

Boulder problems are rated using the V rating, developed at Hueco Tanks by John Sherman, and used internationally for bouldering, it is considered that V0 starts at 5.10, with VB for 5.9 and below (some problems have YDS in parenthesis, this indicates that the route is also top roped). Boulder ratings are very subjective, therefore, the V ratings in the chart have been subdivided into three overlapping categories: EASY - MODERATE - HARD, an adjective for how the problem 'feels' to an expert climber, if you think I've over or underrated a problem bear this in mind, also bear in mind that the opinions polled from the regulars may be a little skewed by familiarity.

SAFETY NOTES
Problems with an 'R' have either a highball crux, a bad landing, or a mix of these, so beware! Lack of an 'R' does not imply that a problem is safe, remember that bouldering by nature is dangerous and can lead to injury or even death. Always use a spotter(s) and crash pad.

QUALITY RATING SYSTEM
★★★ Stoney Classic
★★ A very good climb
★ A better than average climb

AMENITIES
There are none in the park (no water, or toilets), so leave home prepared.

V and three international systems compared

	V	YDS	Fb	UK
Easy	VB	5.7 5.8 5.9	5	4c 5a
	V0	5.10a 5.10b 5.10c 5.10d	6a	5b 5c
	V1	5.11a 5.11b 5.11c 5.11d	6b	6a
	V2			
	V3			
Moderate	V4	5.12a 5.12b 5.12c 5.12d	6c	6b
	V5			
	V6		7a	6c
	V7	5.13a 5.13b 5.13c 5.13d		7a
	V8		7b	
Hard	V9			
	V10	5.14a	7c	7b
	V11	5.14b		
	V12	5.14c	8a	7b
	V13	5.14d		

V = Vermin
YDS = Yosemite Decimal Standard (USA)
Fb = Fontainbleu (France)
UK = United Kingdom

WEATHER

It's possible to climb at Stoney Point all year round, although it can get a little hot in the summer.

Do not climb when the routes are wet or immediately after it's rained!

Wait for at least 3 days of fine weather before climbing; water saturated into the porous rock seriously weakens it.

HEINOUS ACTS

Trash: Let's face it, Stoney Point is trashed. Please try to take out some trash while you are here (clean and climb) and discourage people from being untidy (climbers included). Try to help if there are any clean up activities being held. Cleaning activities are announced at *http://www.sowr.com.*

Graffiti: Look at the recent pictures of *Hot Tuna* on Pages 2-3, now check out Mike Waugh on the same problem in *Stone Crusade (by John Sherman)*, notice any difference?..There's no graffiti on the more recent shots thanks to the work of climbers in cooperation with Recreation and Parks. This was achieved by lightly spraying over the mess with rock colored paint, the paint is sufficiently thin enough to allow the rock to stay rough. Contact Mark Meyer of Recreation and Parks to request free equipment and supplies. *Together we can make a difference.*

Chipping: *Chipping is cheating* and it's happening at an alarming rate. Problems that even I can do have been chipped. If you can't get the problem, work out, get strong and try again. Repeat the dose until you succeed, one day you'll thank me for this advice.

Breaking Holds: Hi, I'm Chris Owen and I've broken holds off classic routes. There I've said it. This happens all too often, remember a few simple rules; never pull out on a hold, only down. Climb light not heavy, with an emphasis on feet, not arms. Don't dyno if you don't have to. Don't climb after it rains. Don't hang from holds. *Protect the climbs for future generations.* If a hold breaks off *DON'T CHIP A NEW ONE!* You might not be able to get it, but someone will.

CREEPY CRAWLIES

The nearest emergency room is at Northridge Medical Center.

Nasties here include Poison Oak, Rattlers, Black Widows, and Bees.

There is a lot of Poison Oak on the north side learn to recognize it; a group of 3 slick shiny leaves gives it away - don't touch it! If you do you'll get a rash a few days later. This stuff spreads so wash all of your clothes etc..

If a snake bites you, relax. Walk to your car and go to the emergency room.

Black Widows often set up camp in potholes (huecos) so check before you reach in.

Africanized Bees are very aggressive, don't go near them on a warm day, and if they get angry, run.

CORRESPONDENCE & OTHER RESOURCES

Information can be found, or comments can be posted on the Mountain Project Stoney Point page: *http://www.mountainproject.com/v/stoney-point/105870979*

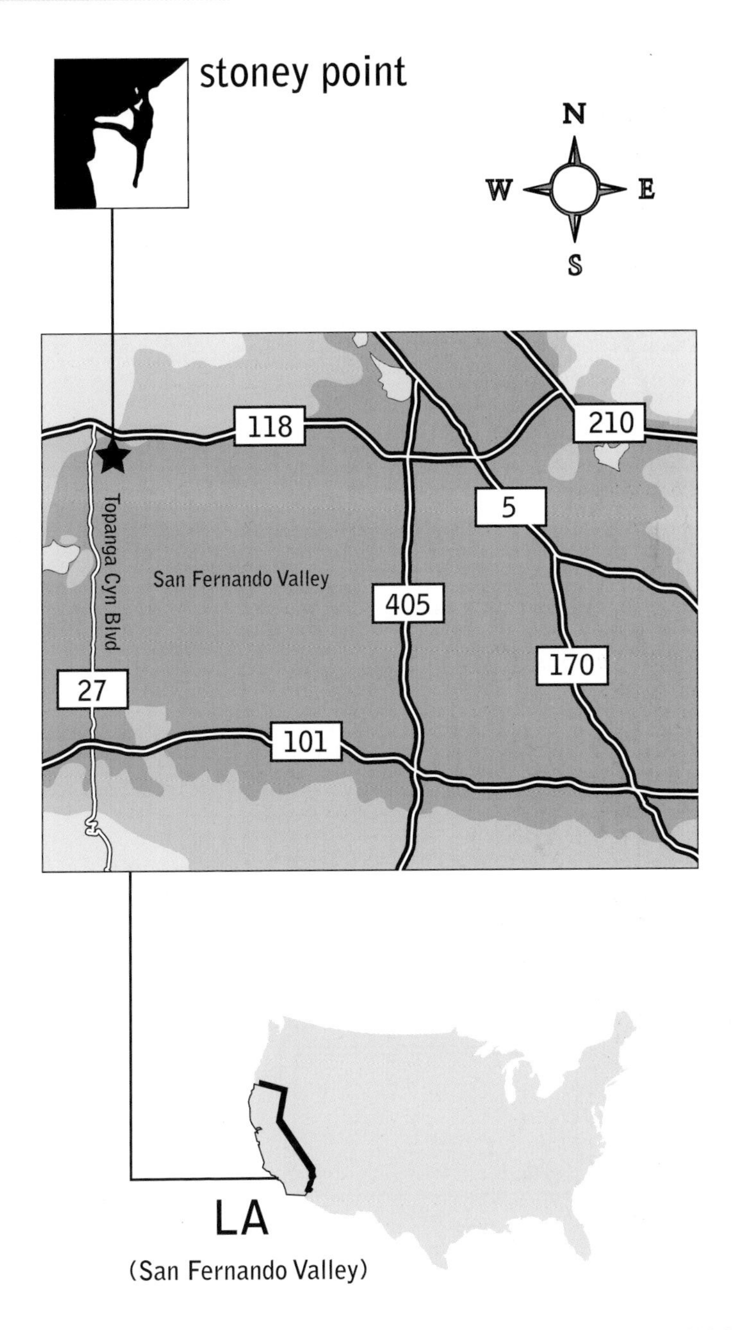

LOCATION MAP

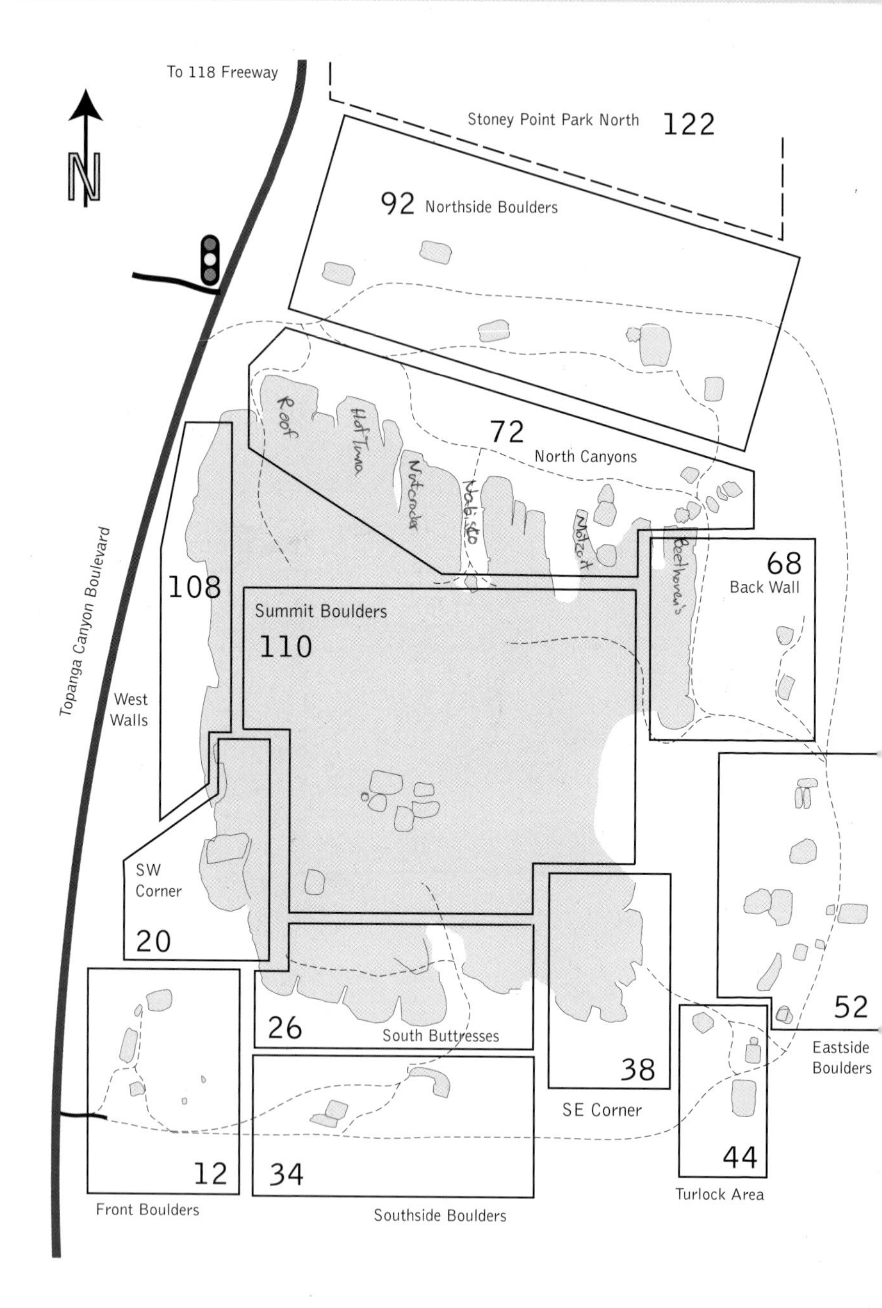

MAP OF STONEY POINT

Go to the page number indicated to find a more detailed area map.

front boulders

Scott Nomi relaxes on Three Pigs V0 (Page 15)

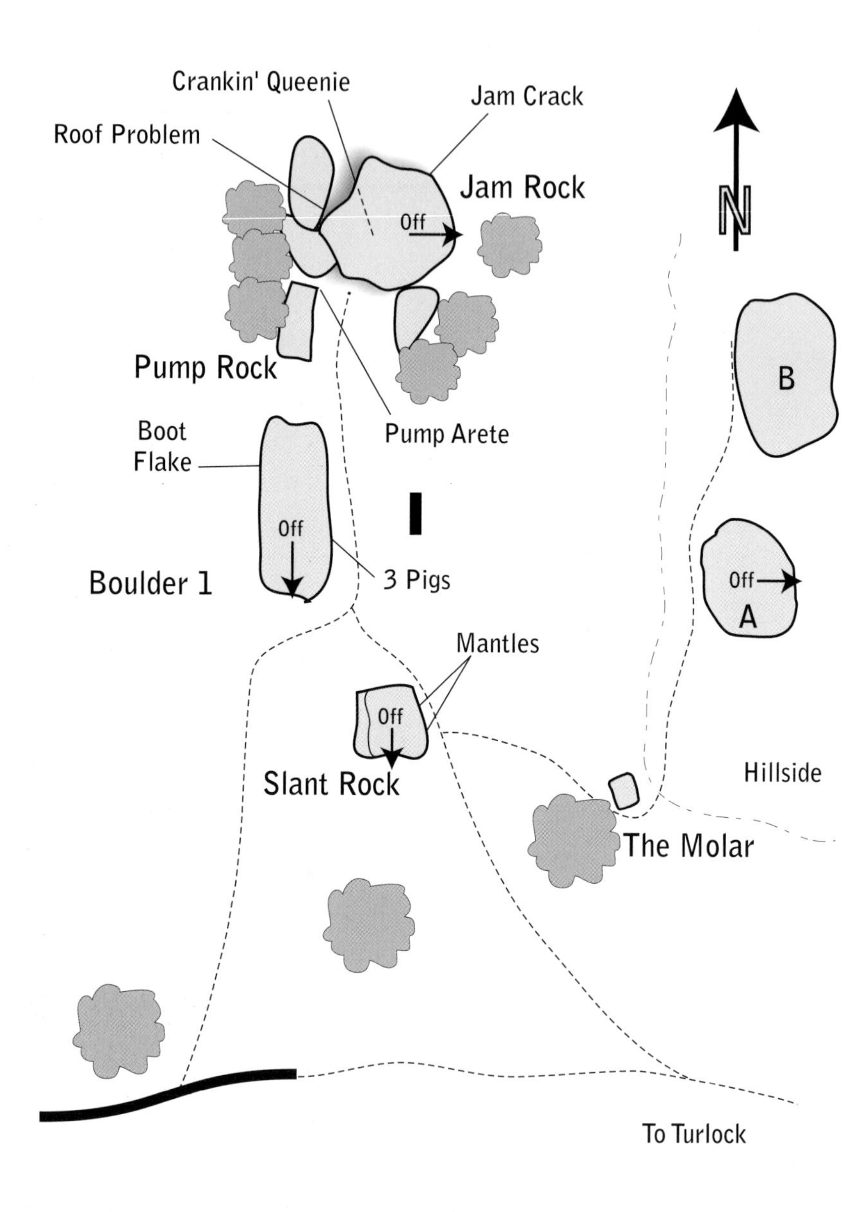

FRONT BOULDERS

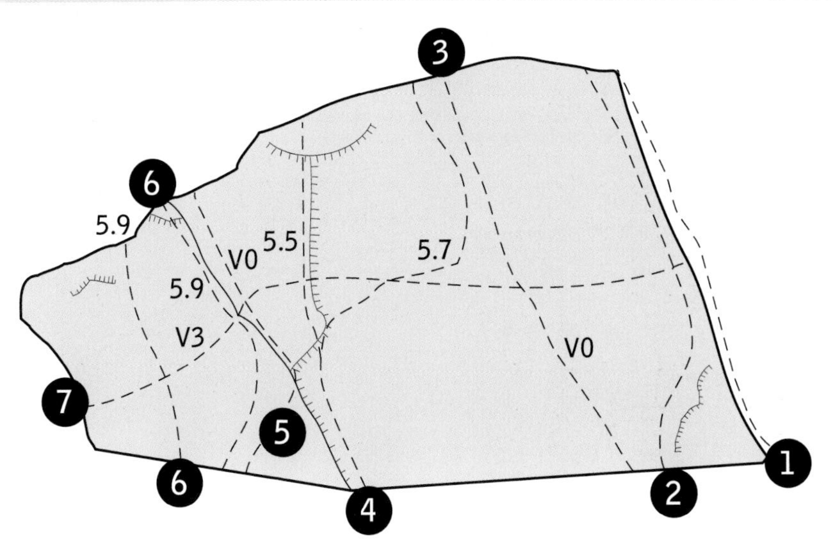

Slant Rock

A good place for beginners and kids (don't laugh, tomorrow they'll kick your butt).

1. **THE SLAB** VB
   Graded for using hands, try it without.
2. **THE EDGE** VB
   This is fun no-handed.
3. **NORTH SIDE RH★** V0
   Thin edging and smearing to a mantle.
4. **NORTH SIDE LH** VB
   Large flakes. Or go right and up the face.
5. **ARETE★** V0
   Start at the Right Mantle but pull around rightward, on the arete, then up on slopers, Route 4 is off.
6. **MANTLES** V0
   The right hand one is a little harder, variations include starting low and dynoing.
7. **TRAVERSE★** V3
   From left to right is a lot harder than the other way and involves a blind lunge for a sidepull.

Nikki Reardon on Three Pigs V0 (Page 15)
Michael Reardon Collection

Boulder 1

The traditional meeting place. A rather large social scene can be experienced here on a summer's eve. A fellow boulderer once told me that he came here to climb one evening and spent 2 hours talking!

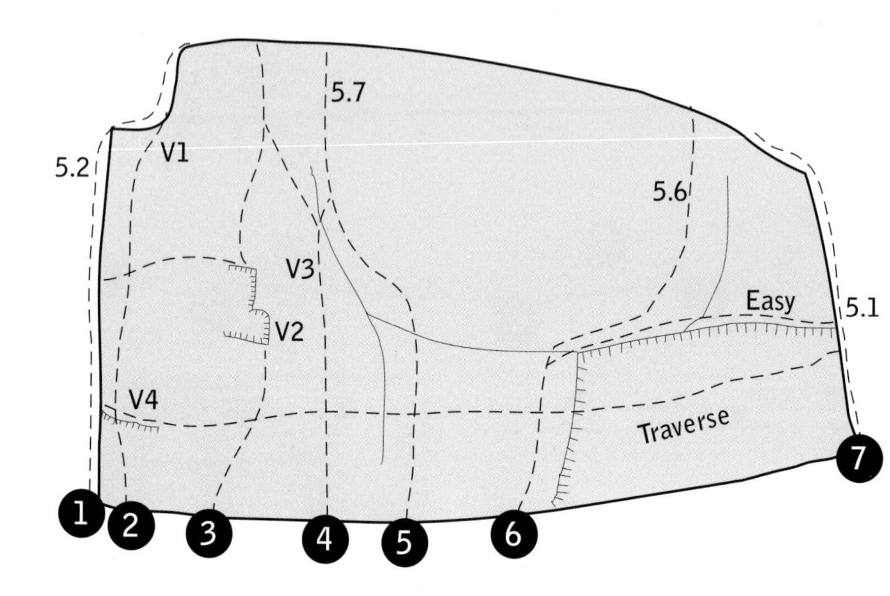

West Side

Although the east side of this boulder is usually done unroped, the west side is a little taller and a top rope can be helpful especially for beginners. The top of the boulder can be reached by climbing East Face Route; bolts and nuts make up the anchor. Route length 25′.

❶ WEST ARETE★★ VB
The arete is steep, yet has good holds.

❷ NYLON BOY★★★ V1
A line of flakes leads up the wall to the left of Boot Flake, resist temptation to swing onto the west Arete.

❸ BOOT FLAKE★★★ V2
The crux is reaching the flake, although the moves above are committing and not easy. A variation (DOUBLE-DYNO★★★ V6) can also be climbed by dynoing for the Boot, then the top of Boulder 1.

❹ ENDO BOY★★★ V3
Steep and crimpy then join Short Story or left to Boot Flake (better and more sustained).

❺ SHORT STORY★★ VB
Getting past the sloping ledge near the top is the crux.

❻ VIVARIN★ VB
After gaining a ledge step right. The wall above is the crux.

❼ EAST FACE ROUTE VB
A tough start leads to better holds, the standard descent route.

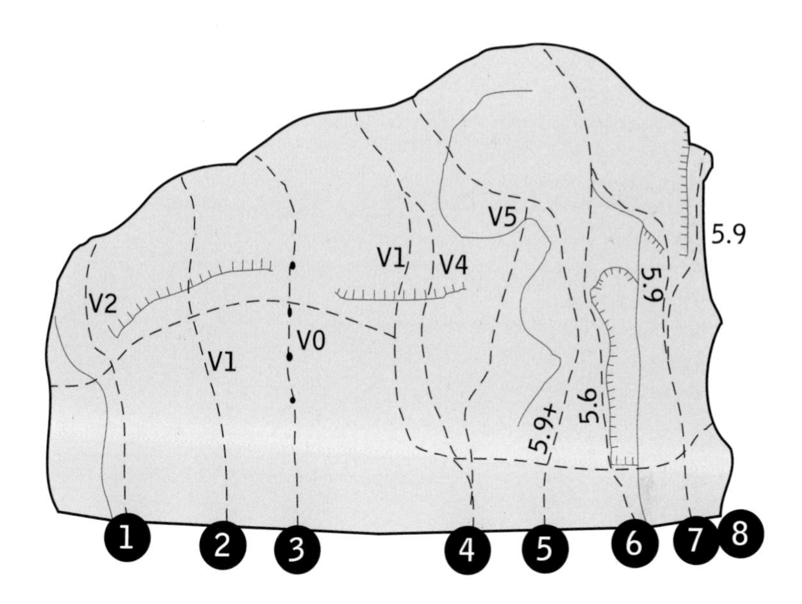

East Side

Generally speaking the problems have polished holds - but there are some classics here.

BOULDER 1 TRAVERSE★★★ V4
North and south are rest areas, the remainder is mostly steep and fingery, especially the NW corner if you stay low.

❶ SE CORNER★ V2
The start is very balancy, the head straight up. As a variation it's possible to go right along the undercling (easier).

❷ 10-40 V1
A reachy start leads to the undercling, going over this requires nerve.

❸ THREE PIGS★ V0
"Your 1st 5.10". The pinscars are only good when you pull sideways. As a variation ignore the pinscars... V2, or do a sit start, variations abound.

❹ UNDERCLING V1
Reach the undercling via weird moves. A chopped hold up and right might give you courage to go. A superior variation (**YABO MANTLE★★** V4) eliminates the chopped hold. (**VAINO'S DYNO★★** V6) shoots for the mantle from the sidepulls. Another variation (**LEAPING LIZARDS★★** V5) shoots for a big flat hold over to the right just before the angle eases using the same sidepulls.

❺ NOSE ELIMINATE★★ V0
Reachy at the start, head straight up on small holds.

❻ THE NOSE★★★ VB
Either lieback it or come up from the right, then climb up the slab.

❼ DIHEDRAL LEFT V0
Exit left with help from pinscars.

❽ DIHEDRAL RIGHT V0
Exit right using a committing reach for the lip.

Pump Rock

Just north of Boulder 1, on the left of the corridor leading to Jam Rock.

❶ THE PUMP TRAVERSE★★ V1
If you're tall it's tougher, start off on the left about an inch from the ground and work your way up and right, and along the east side then turn the last corner and mantle up.

TRUE MANTLE★ V1
On the east side, jump for the lip at about where the face is at its highest; mantle up.

PUMP ARETE★ V1
(See Page 12) Side pulls and body English, throw left for lip, add a sit start, harder.

NORTH FACE MANTLE★ V0
(Right of Pump Arete). Good holds lead to a throw then mantle.

RIGHT ARETE★ V1
Lieback up the north face's right arete.

Jam Rock

On the north side is a good beginner's jam crack, slings are good for the anchor if TR-ing this route. Get to the top by using the East Face. Route length 20'.

❷ WEST FACE★ VB
Walk past Pump Rock then just before the entrance to the cave, make an awkward move onto the boulder which Jam Rock sits on, then transfer to the west face of Jam Rock.

❸ AFTERSHOCK★★ V7
Undercling to a hand match, then a dyno for an iffy sidepull (or sloper).

❹ SOUTH FACE V0R
Easy but highball, with a nasty landing.

CRANKIN' QUEENIE★★ V8R
(See Page 12) From a sit start in the middle, traverse right to polished holds, then up and back left. Top out straight up, or traverse left at the jugs and continue up and over the block at the left side (do not step onto the block, scary). Without the sit start: V4.

ROOF V4
(See Page 12) In the cave on a boulder at 4 o'clock from Crankin' Queenie, close to the ground, roof flakes lead to a mantle.

THE JAM CRACK★★ VB
(See Page 12) On the north side of Jam Rock, try this with jamming technique only.

FACE★ VB
Up the face to the right of the Jam Crack using side pulls and over the little roof.

Other Boulders

ARETE V2
Starts at the same place as Route 2. The left trending 45° rounded arete of the boulder upon which Jam Rock rests.

FACE V0
Start to the left of the previous route, a short face leads to a sloper finish.

❺ SAY GOODNIGHT★ V6
A hard problem on the Matterhorn shaped boulder south of Jam Rock, height dependent, the right edge and left boulder are off.

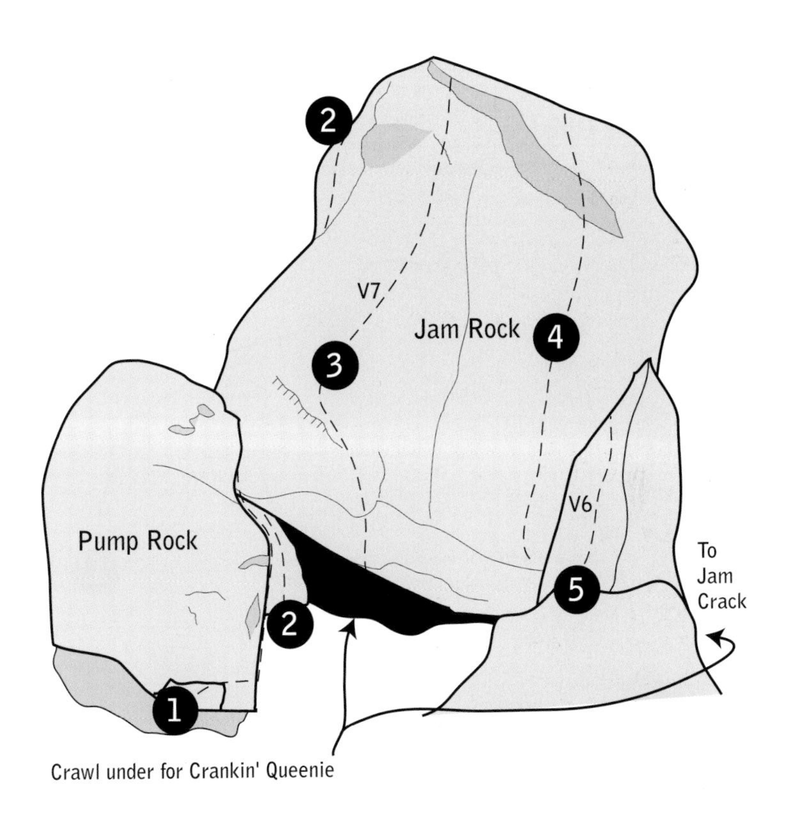

Paul Anderson cranks Crankin' Queenie V8R | Michael Reardon Collection

The Molar (aka Wilson's Mantles)

This small boulder lies to the east of Slant Rock, there are quite a few variations to the mantle moves ranging from 5.8 to V1.

Boulders on the Hillside

Through the brush to the left of The Molar, there are two boulders, with sloping landings, good spotters can he prevent a tumble.

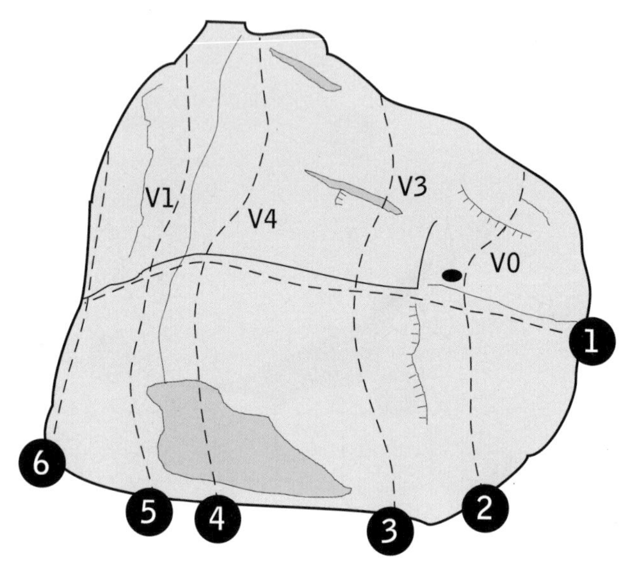

Boulder A

❶ TRAVERSE★ V3
Hand rail, start on the right, pass around the arete and continue.

❷ FACE★ V0
Hole, then finish right on small holds, starts off okay, then surprises you.

❸ ARETE RIGHT★ V1
Bulge followed by attention getting sloper finish.

❹ ARETE DIRECT★ V2
Okay, no more lolly-gagging, 'cat up' for the obvious challenge and tackle the bulge directly.

❺ ARETE LEFT★ V1
High step right on sloper, then long reach for the good hold.

❻ LEFT FACE V0
Gritty face.

Boulder B

There are a number of short, gritty, face climbs here, from the north west face rightward, the problems, in gene al, get tougher -- V0 to V4.

southwest corner

Melody Wong gets some exposure on Rainbow's End 5.10d (Page 24)

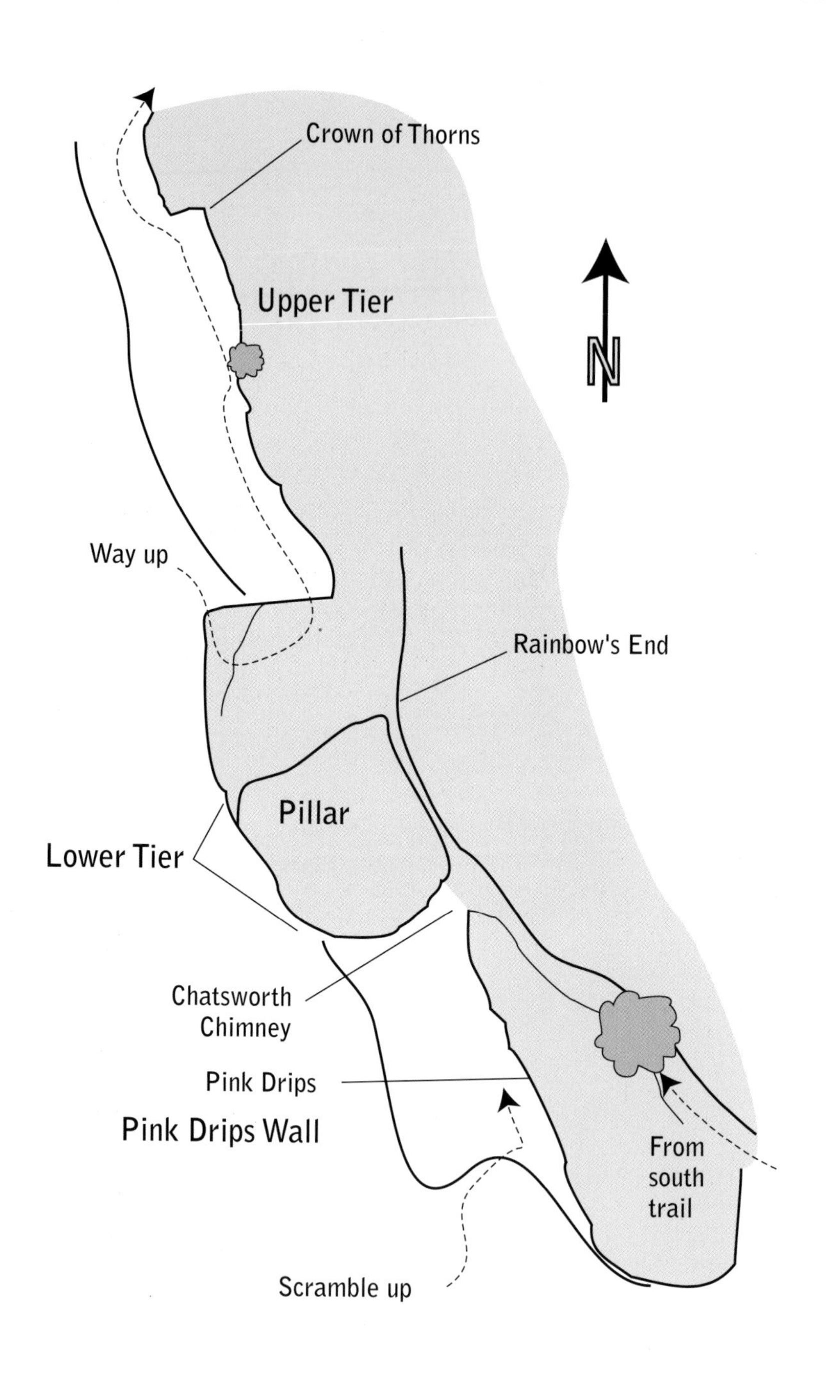

SOUTHWEST CORNER

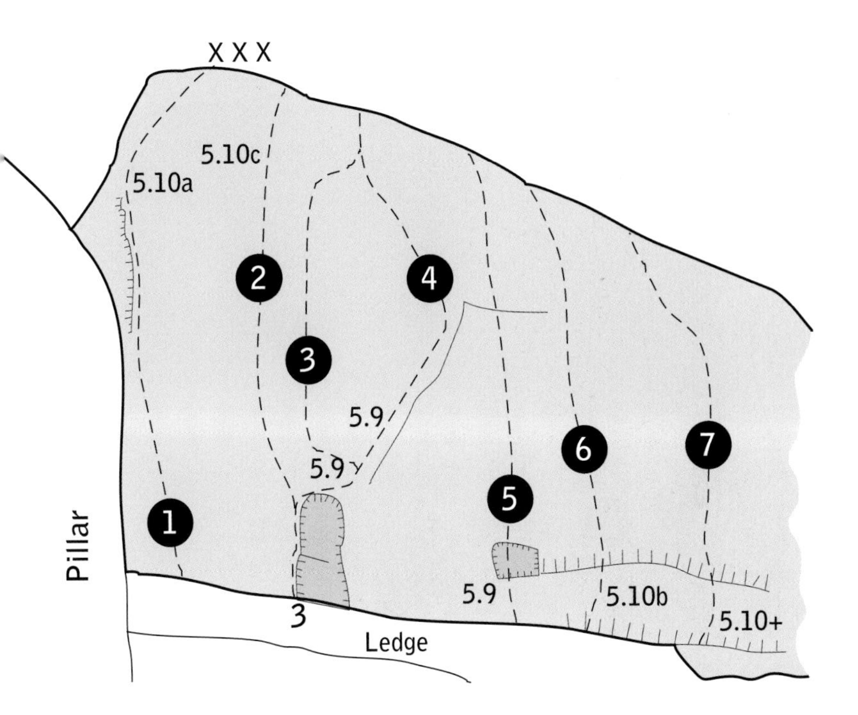

ink Drips Wall

is wall features really good steep face climbing of varying difficulty as well as some overhang problems on the ght. There is a three-bolt anchor on top, as the tree was destroyed by fire.
proach is by a ledge which runs past the bottom of Spencer's Slab and above the South Buttresses. Route ngth 50'.

LEFT ARETE★ 5.10a
Climb just to the right of Chatsworth Chimney, lay off a right facing rib and finish up a fingery wall.

DIRECT★★ 5.10b/c
This lies immediately left of Pink Drips, finish straight up using small but positive holds.

PINK DRIPS★★★ 5.9
A classic face climb; stepping left at the beginning is the crux but don't underestimate the worrying finish.

RIGHT-HAND ROUTE★ 5.9
Instead of going left head up the shallow depression and finish with Pink Drips.

THE BRACKET★ 5.9
A nose of rock sticks out of the face, get on top of it then head straight up. Or pass it on the left.

UNDERWORLD★★ 5.10b
Dynos lead to a wall with a deep pocket, the crux is gaining the small ledge above.

WOUNDED KNEE★★ 5.10d
Gain a sloping ledge; a real puzzler, step left into a depression then climb the wall above. Both of these climbs end on an easy angled section before the top.

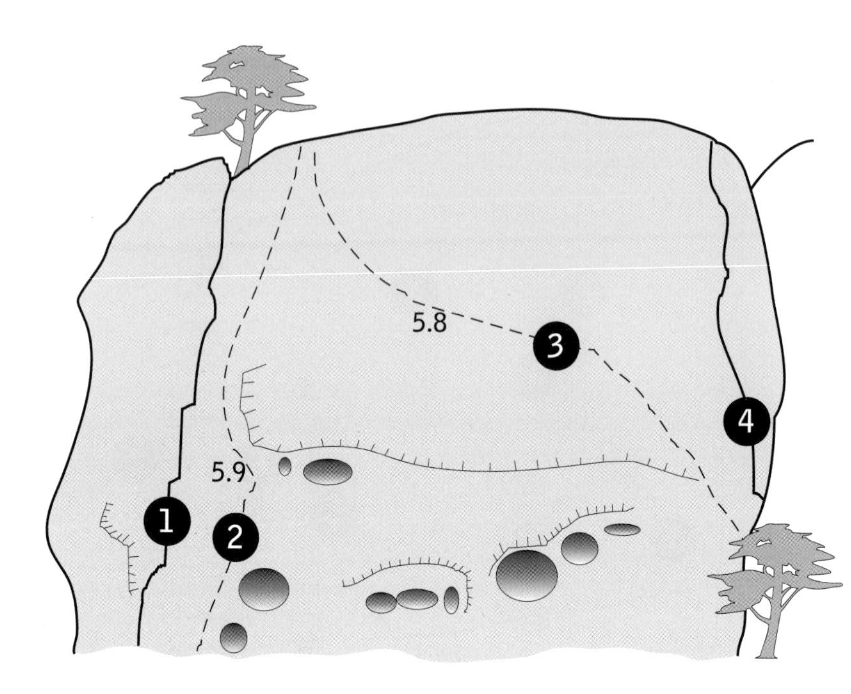

Lower Tier

This is the wall below The Pillar. It features two crack climbs and two face climbs. These routes end where The Pillar routes start. Use tricky cam placements for the anchor set up or use the anchor on The Pillar and combine them with those routes. Route length 35′.

❶ FLAKY CRACK★ 5.7
This crack can be led with great care.

❷ TIERDROP★ 5.9
Climb right of the crack up some interesting, if a little loose, overlaps.

❸ SLAB ROUTE 5.8
Start up the right edge then head up and left over a slab.

❹ RIGHT-HAND CRACK 5.8
Gain the crack from the right edge and follow it to the ledge. Very loose.

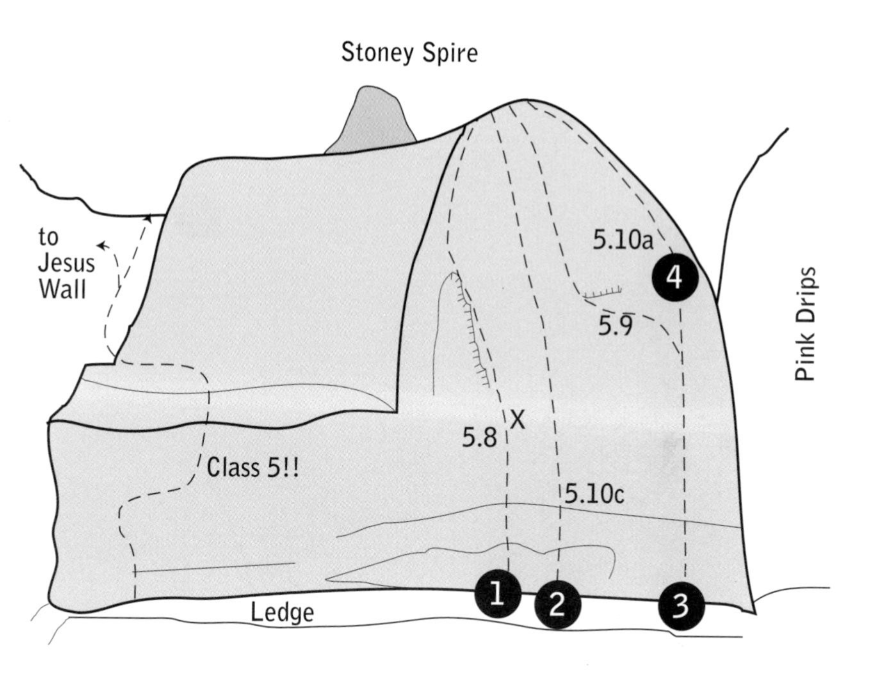

The Pillar

This buttress is located to the left of Pink Drips. Four climbs can be done using one anchor, which consists of two rivets (take wires) and cam placements or a long, long sling over the pinnacle (Stoney Spire) behind the buttress. Route length 45′.

The top is gained by climbing up the broken buttress which forms an abutment between the Jesus Wall and The Pillar. Head up a steep tricky little wall then traverse right to Stoney Spire.

1 THE CRACK 5.8R
Loose flake. The crux is stepping left past the bolt; use the flake above with great care! Lead it if you dare.

2 MANTLEPEACE★ 5.10c
A nasty mantle leads to a steep face.

3 PILLAR LEFT★ 5.9
Up loose holds then left over an overlap.

4 PILLAR RIGHT★ 5.10a
Go right then teeter up a slab.

CHATSWORTH CHIMNEY 5.7
This is located between The Pillar and Pink Drips Wall. Up the chimney then go right and up a trough to finish on top of Pink Drips. Can be led.

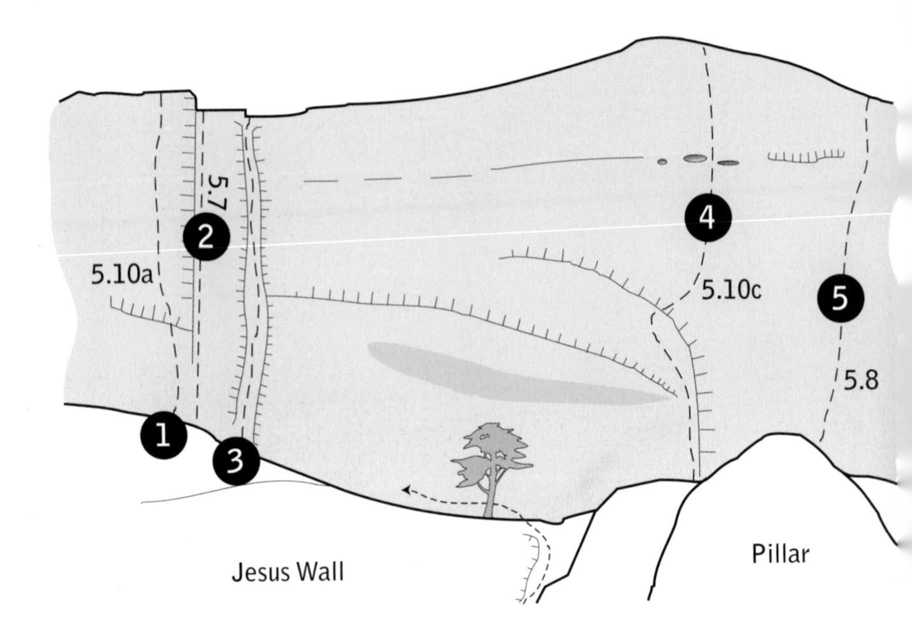

Upper Tier

Above The Pillar there is a wall with some arches on its left side, this is the Upper Tier. To reach the top, either climb up the broken buttress to the right of The Jesus Wall, then up and left over ledges, or go around the south side of Stoney Point and head up past Spencer's Slab. Nuts and long slings provide the anchors. Route length 30'/40'.

❶ POCKET ROCKET★ 5.10a
Up the overhanging wall using pockets.

❷ CROWN OF THORNS★★ 5.7
Short but sweet. Gain the obvious open book then lieback to the top finishing with a tricky mantle move.

❸ ARCH CHIMNEY 5.5
The weakness to the right of Crown of Thorns.

❹ RAINBOW'S END★★ 5.10+
A very exposed climb, use the pin scarred crack to get over the overlap. The crux is climbing the very steep wall above.

❺ STUDLEY SLAB 5.8
This takes the face with the bolt studs in it.

south buttresses

Tony Tennessee hangs out on the roof of Eye of Faith 5.10c (Page 29)

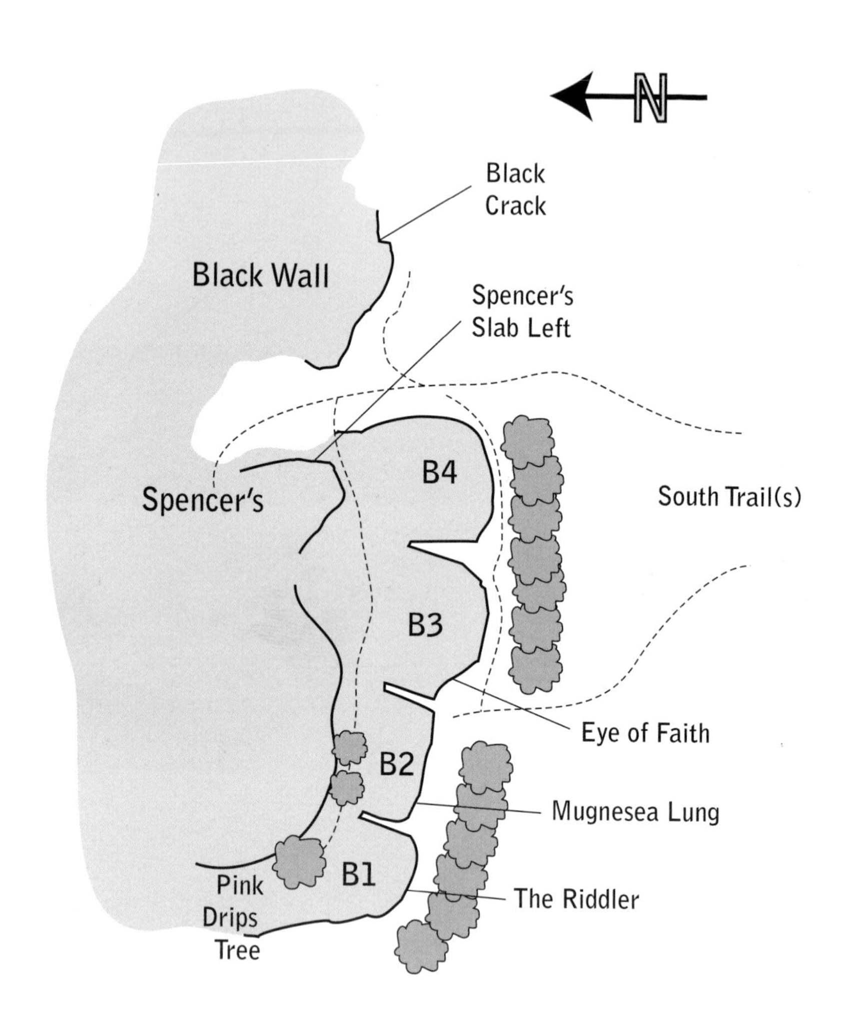

SOUTH BUTTRESSES

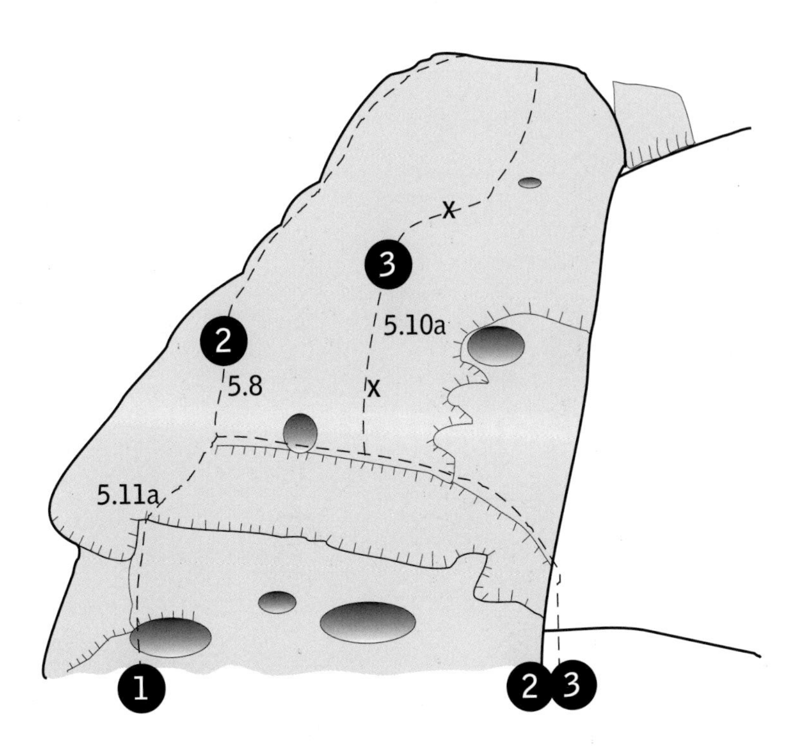

Buttress #1

This buttress is actually the right hand edge of the Pink Drips Wall. Use the Pink Drips tree for an anchor. It may also be possible to use some nuts/cams in the cracks by the chockstone. Route length 50′.

1 BATMAN AND OWEN★ 5.11a
Another overhang. Gain the niche below a roof, pull over the roof using finger pockets and follow the easier arete to the top.

2 THE RIDDLER★★ 5.8
Gain the same arete by traversing in from the chimney to the right. The crux is a mantle on to a knob.

3 BOLTED LEAD 5.10aR
Follow the bolts up the face to the right of the arete.

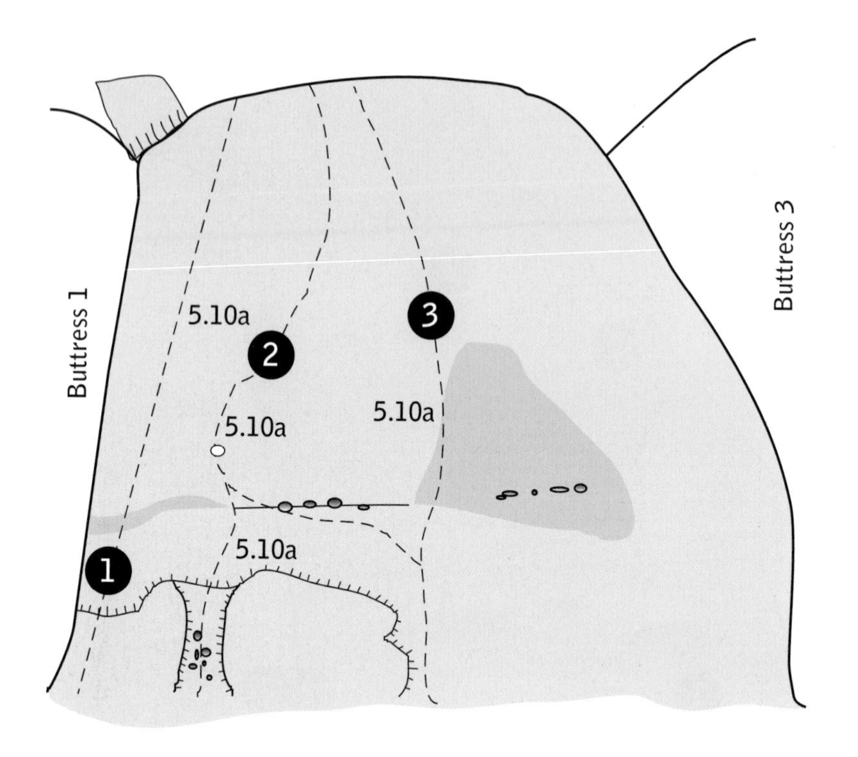

Buttress #2

Some of the better slab climbs at Stoney are located on this buttress. The Pink Drips tree and nuts/cams make up the anchor. Take care not to get the rope snagged on an expansion bolt sleeve sticking out of the slab near the top.
Route length 40′.

1 CHOCKSTONE WALL 5.10a
A line can be found to the right of the chimney.

2 MUGNESEA LUNG★★ 5.10a
Once upon a time this route was a lead, the bolts are widely spaced and very bad, it's best to TR. Climb delicately just left of the front of the slab.

3 SAVAGE SLAB★★ 5.10a
Another delicate climb which heads up the front of the slab and eventually joins the left route.

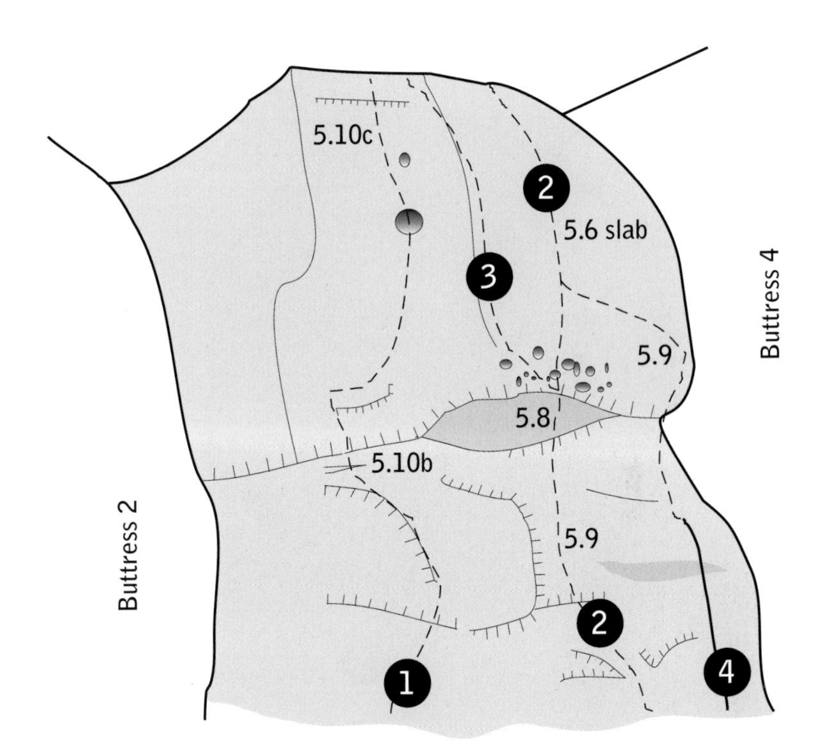

Buttress #3

he roof routes on this buttress should not be missed. They are both classics. For the anchor sling a boulder and se some nuts/cams in a crack on the right. Route length 45′.

1 EYE OF FAITH★★★ 5.10c
A great route. Pull up over the roof and climb up the wall, past "The Eye", to a belly flop finale.

2 PAUL'S HOLE (AKA GEORGE'S OVERHANG)★★★ 5.9
The crux is getting up to the overhang. Avoid any temptation to crawl into the hole. Pull and stem over the overhang. The slab above is sheer delight.

3 CONNECTIONS★ 5.9
It's possible to leave Paul's Hole above the overhang and climb up the faint rib to the right of Eye Of Faith.

4 NOW VOYAGER 5.9
This starts at the bottom of Paul's Hole but wanders to the right up over a steep section, then joins the top slab.

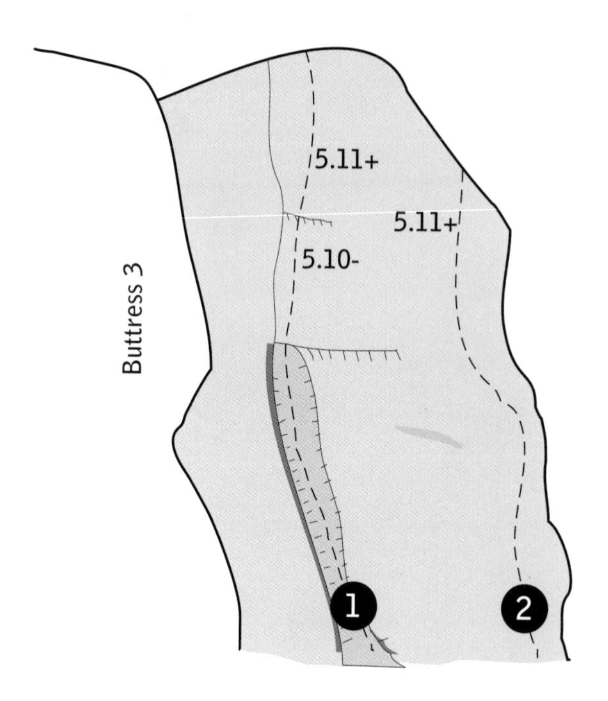

Buttress #4

This buttress gets steep at the top and the holds all but disappear. A boulder sitting on top provides an anchor. Watch out for broken glass beneath it. Route length 50′.

1 SEMIDETACHED★★ 5.11+
Go up the rib which rests on the buttress, past a tricky step, then up on very small holds (crux). A couple of palmy moves lead to the top.

2 RIGHT ROUTE 5.11+
Up a slab, loose, then, when the wall steepens, move to the left (ignoring the chopped holds on the right) and make very thin technical moves to the top.

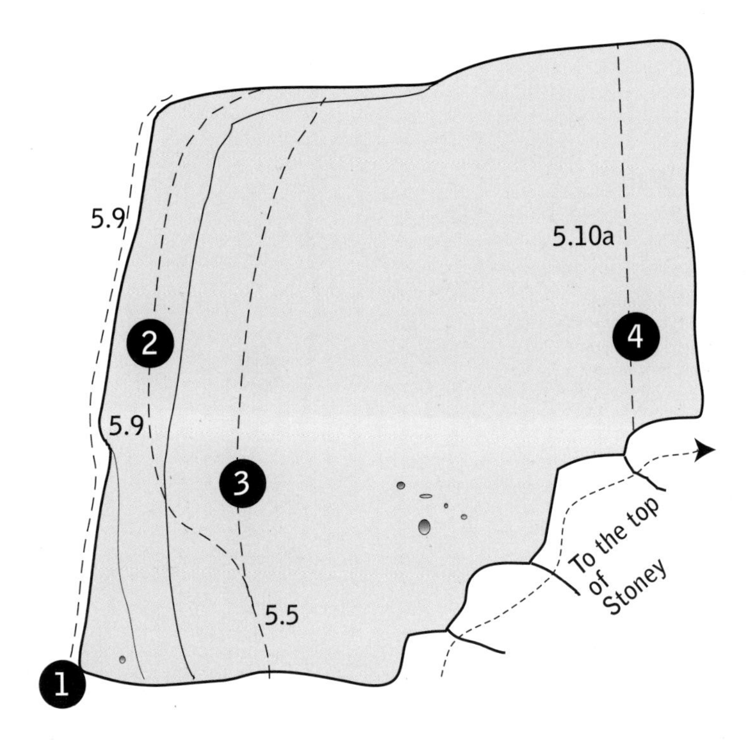

Spencer's Slab

This is located above Buttress #4 and has an easy slab climb in a good position. Nuts and slings provide an anchor. There are bolt studs too. Route length 35′.

1. FRONT ROUTE 5.9
   The front pocketed face.
2. OFFSET SLAB★ 5.10a
   Start at the main slab, then go left and climb the subsidiary one.
3. SPENCER'S SLAB LEFT★★ 5.5
   A good climb up the left of the slab.
4. SPENCER'S SLAB RIGHT★ 5.10a
   The blank slab on the right.

The Black Wall

This is located to the right of the south side trail to the top of Stoney. Slings, nuts and trees provide an anchor. Route length 35′.

1 THE BLACK WALL
(aka NOSE CONE)★★★ 5.11a
The overhanging wall provides an exciting exercise in lock offs and long reaches.

2 BLACK CRACK★ 5.9
Climb the dihedral to the right of the previous route, then step left and finish up the wall.

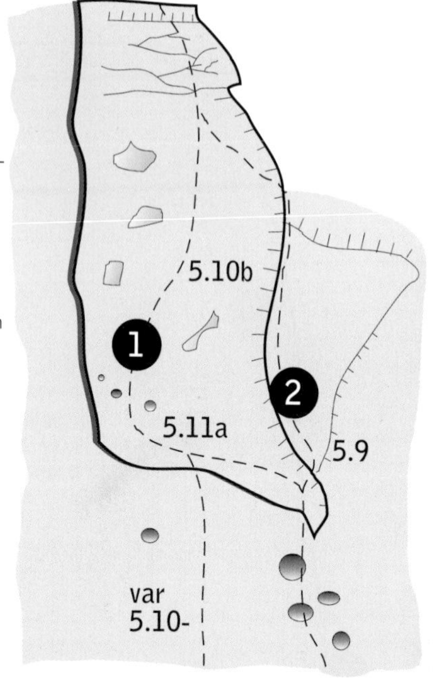

Noreen Flynn tames the Savage Slab 5.10a (Page 28)

southside boulders

Tony Tennessee makes the first snatch of Pile Lieback V2 (Page 35)

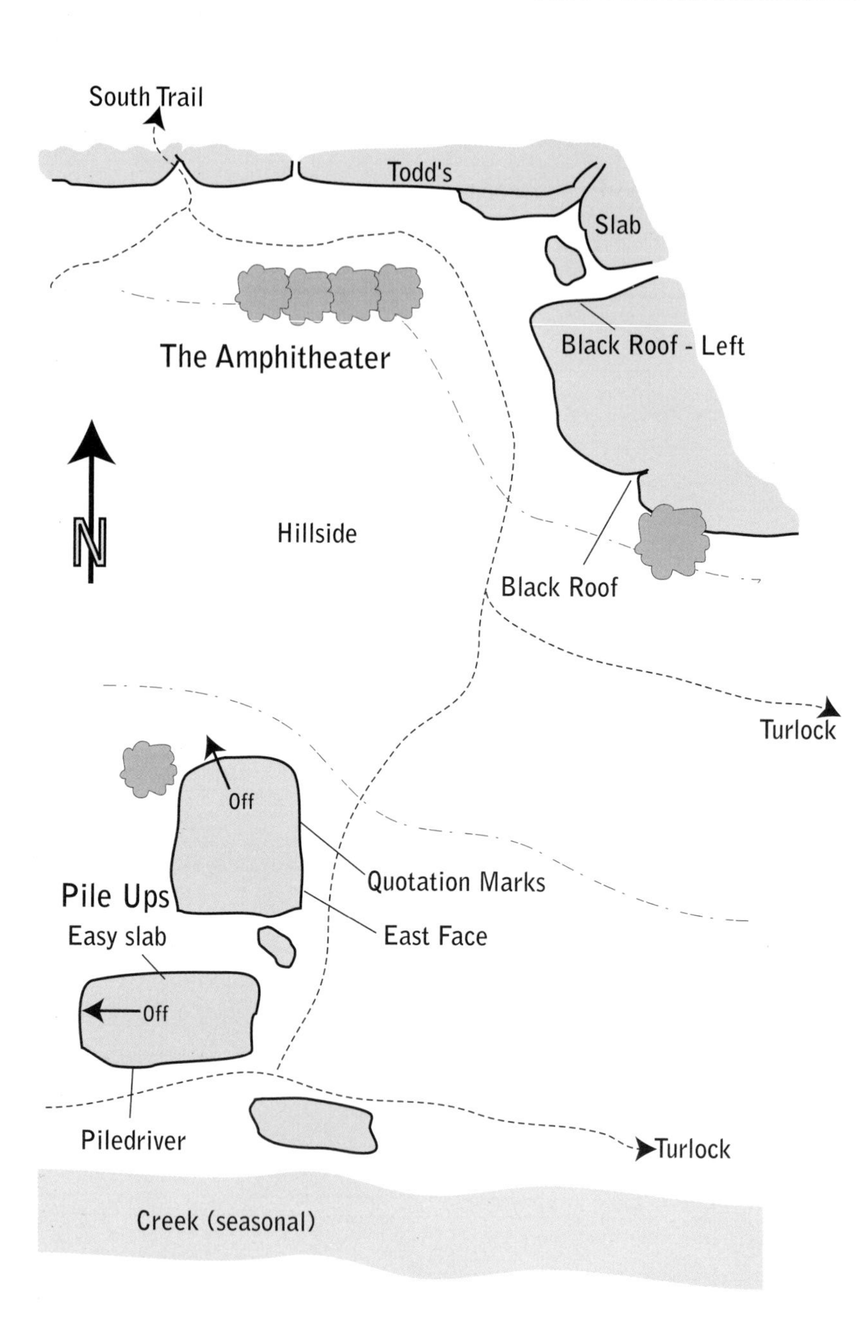

SOUTHSIDE BOULDERS

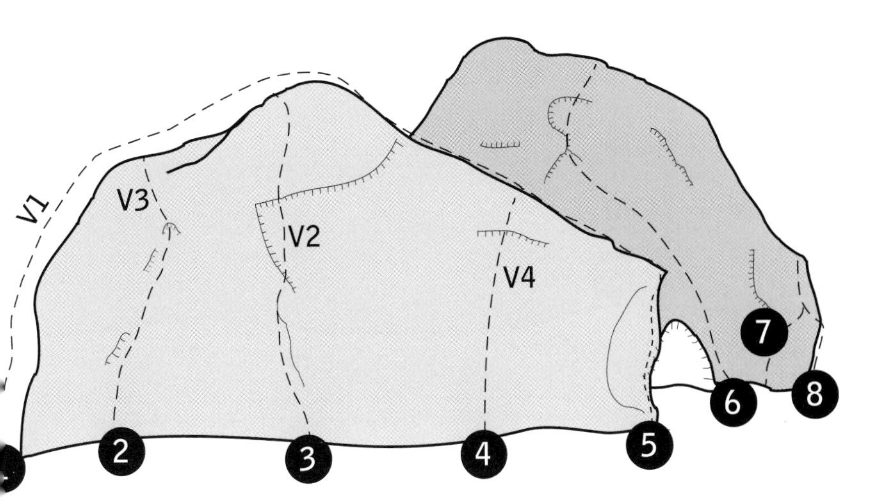

Pile Ups (aka Angel's Wings)

On the left hand side of the trail when walking towards Turlock. Turn left here to find the Amphitheater also. There's a good concentration of moderate boulder problems here, and also some harder variations (not described).

1. LIP TRAVERSE★★ V1
   Hand traverse the lip of the first boulder, then head back.

2. PILEDRIVER★★★ V3
   A very awkward start to a barely adequate crimp (or two), then very powerful pull for sloper and mantle over the lip.

3. PILE LIEBACK★★★ V2
   Polished hold to side pull, lieback, then ledge. Add a sit start for **GOMER PILE★★★** (V4).

4. SLEDGEHAMMER★ V4
   Sloping holds lead to a reasonable ledge.

5. ROOF & MANTLE VB
   Mantle up on the end of the boulder, or try variations without the obvious holds.

6. FACE V2R
   Creepy top out from large flake, bad landing, nowadays it's doable with crashpads.

7. TRAVERSE V3
   Starting holds of previous route traverse right and up to slab finish.

8. SDS V6
   A sit start to the finishing holds of Route 7.

Pile Ups ~ East Face of 2nd Boulder

Some moderate problems and a thin/smeary route provide contrast to the overhanging crimpy stuff.

EAST FACE★ V0
(Page 34). Thin edging and smearing, then left and very palmy to finish up Route 7 or mantle direct, which is a little trickier and involves a committing mantle (V1).

QUOTATION MARKS★ VB
(Page 34). Climb up the face using the pockets, or eliminate the pockets for a tougher (V0) problem.

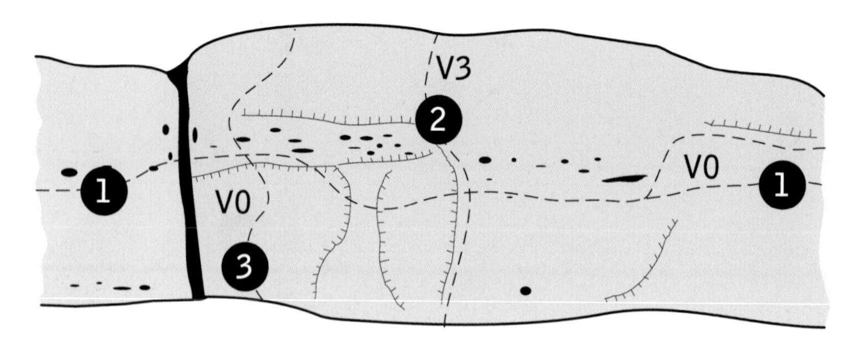

Amphitheater

An excellent easy traverse, plus a number of "up" problems make this a good spot for spending some time. Finishing moves on the up problems are gritty, so watch out.

1 TODD'S TRAVERSE (AKA AMPHITHEATER TRAVERSE)★★★ V0
At first very balancy and then strenuous. From right to left and back again. 12 times is a 1000ft!

LOW TRAVERSE★★ V3
A low traverse, which can run either direction, ignoring all of the larger Todd's holds.

2 PIN SCARS★ V3
The pock marked seam leads to a hairy top out.

3 MIKE'S UP PROBLEM V0
Awkward and strenuous to Todd's, then delicate and grainy to finish.

Scott Nomi rounds the corner of Todd's Traverse V0

Black Roof

SLAB★ VBR
(Page 34). Some smearing and palming moves lead to the ledge. Quite good.

THE BLACK ROOF - LEFT SIDE V3R
(Page 34). Look to the right of the Slab, a face climb up the left side of the roof on iffy holds and a nasty landing.

THE BLACK ROOF★ V0R
(Page 34). Take the roof crack behind the tree, get a solid fist jam. The hard part is pulling over the lip.

southeast corner

Chris Barker is all feet on the crux of Pin Scars 5.9 (Page 41)

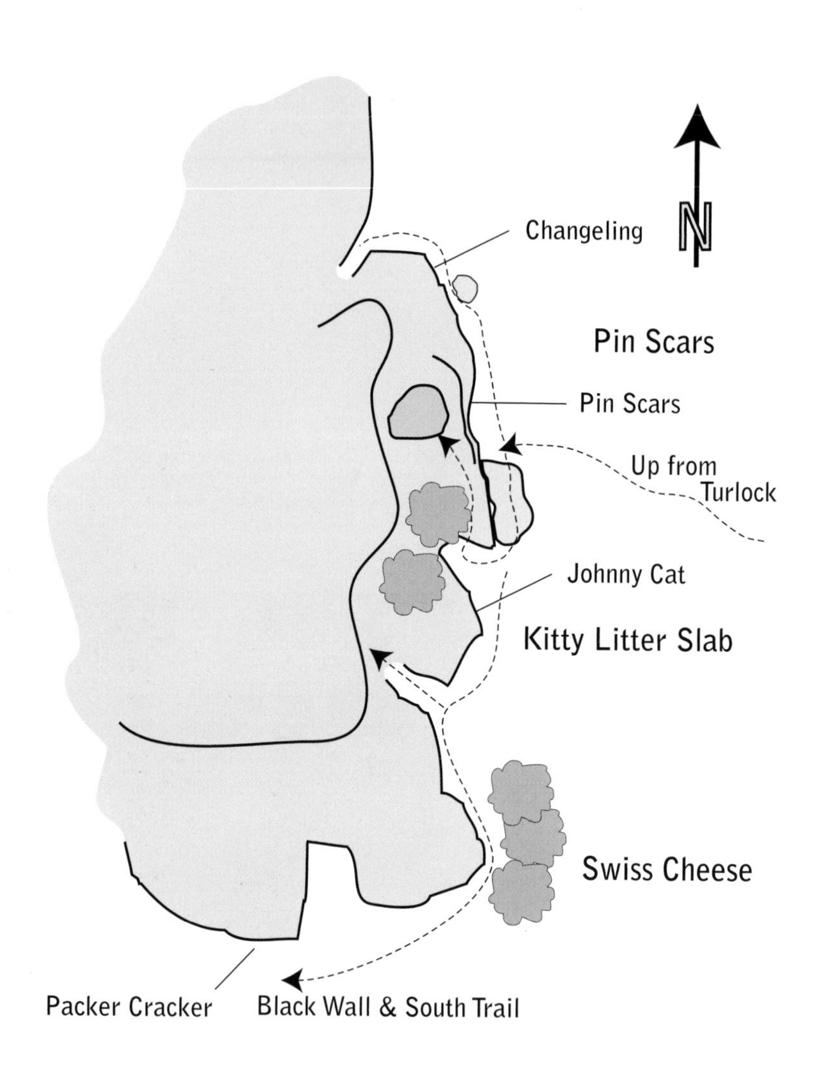

SOUTHEAST CORNER

wiss Cheese Buttress

his is the pocketed wall to the left of Pin Scars. There are some boulders that can be slung for an anchor ehind the top of the buttress. Route length 35′.

PACKER CRACKER V1
(See Page 38). This climb is around the corner to the left. Ascend a curving crack.

1 LEFT ROUTE 5.9+
Steep, loose climbing.

2 RIGHT ROUTE★ 5.9+
Up flakes to a problematical finish either left or right.

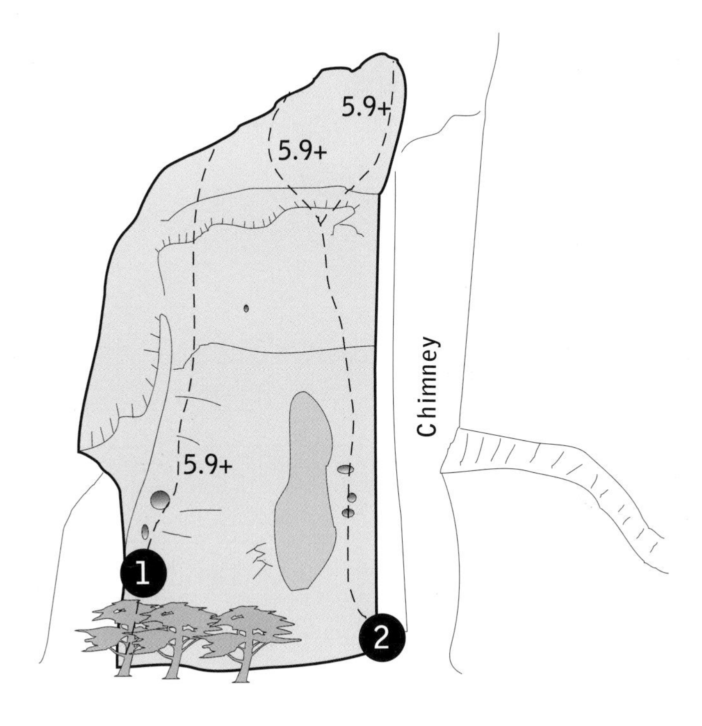

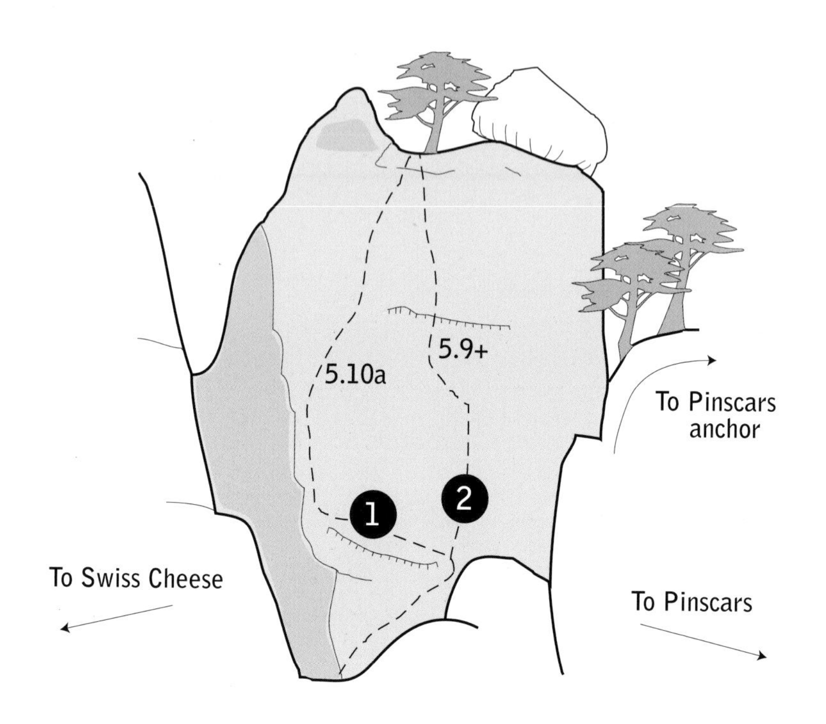

Kitty Litter Slab

Around the corner to the left of Pin Scars is a slab with a triangular roof on the left at the top. To set up the anchor either go up the gully to the left or reach the top from the Pin Scars anchor. Sling a tree. Route length 35′.

❶ TIDY CAT★ 5.10a
Traverse out to the left edge and smear and palm your way to the top.

❷ JOHNNY CAT★ 5.9+
Head straight up the middle of the slab to a foot pedaling mantle followed by easier climbing.

Pin Scars Wall ~ Left Side

The obvious pin scarred cracks on the wall are visible from the trail near Turlock. These climbs, although artificial, are fun and strenuous, and possible in the worst of monsoon conditions!
Sling a boulder on top for the anchor. Route length 40′.

1 SCARFACE★ 5.6
An easy route to the left of the cracks.

2 MAGNUM CASE★ 5.9
Start at the bottom of the wall and climb up the left hand pin scarred crack.

3 PIN SCARS (AKA MACHINE GUN)★★★ 5.9
The right hand crack proves to be strenuous. The crux is getting past the steep section.

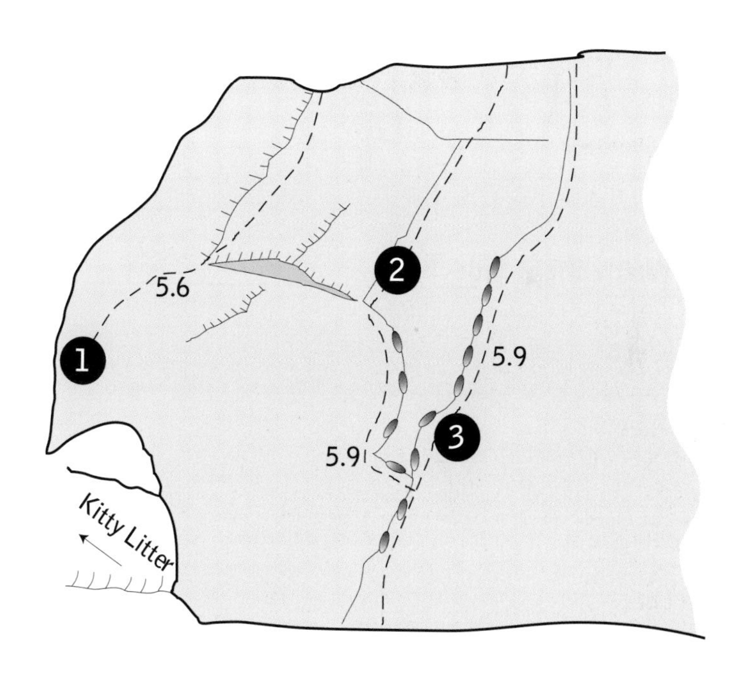

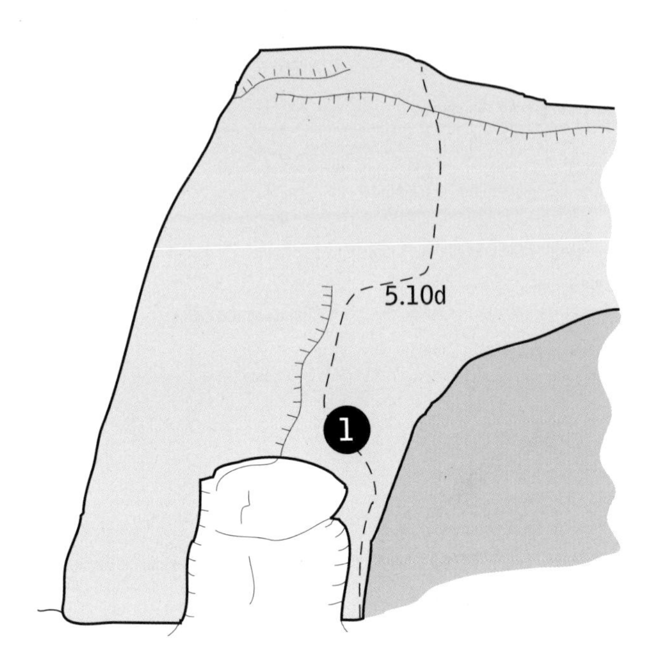

Pin Scars Wall ~ Right Side

❶ CHANGELING★★ 5.10d
This climb is located around the corner to the right. One dyno after another leads to a ledge. Don't relax though, the crux is next; an awkward high step leads to better holds and the top.

THE CHIMNEY 5.5
This is in the corner and is generally soloed.

To the right lie some short walls with V0 problems. Above and to the left of these there is a fun lieback crack which is generally bouldered (5.8). At the top of the Pin Scars Wall is a pinnacle which can be soloed. On a clear winter's day there is a great view of the city with snow-capped mountains from here.

turlock area

Bob Kamps on The Ear circa 1965 (Page 48) | Bob Kamps Collection

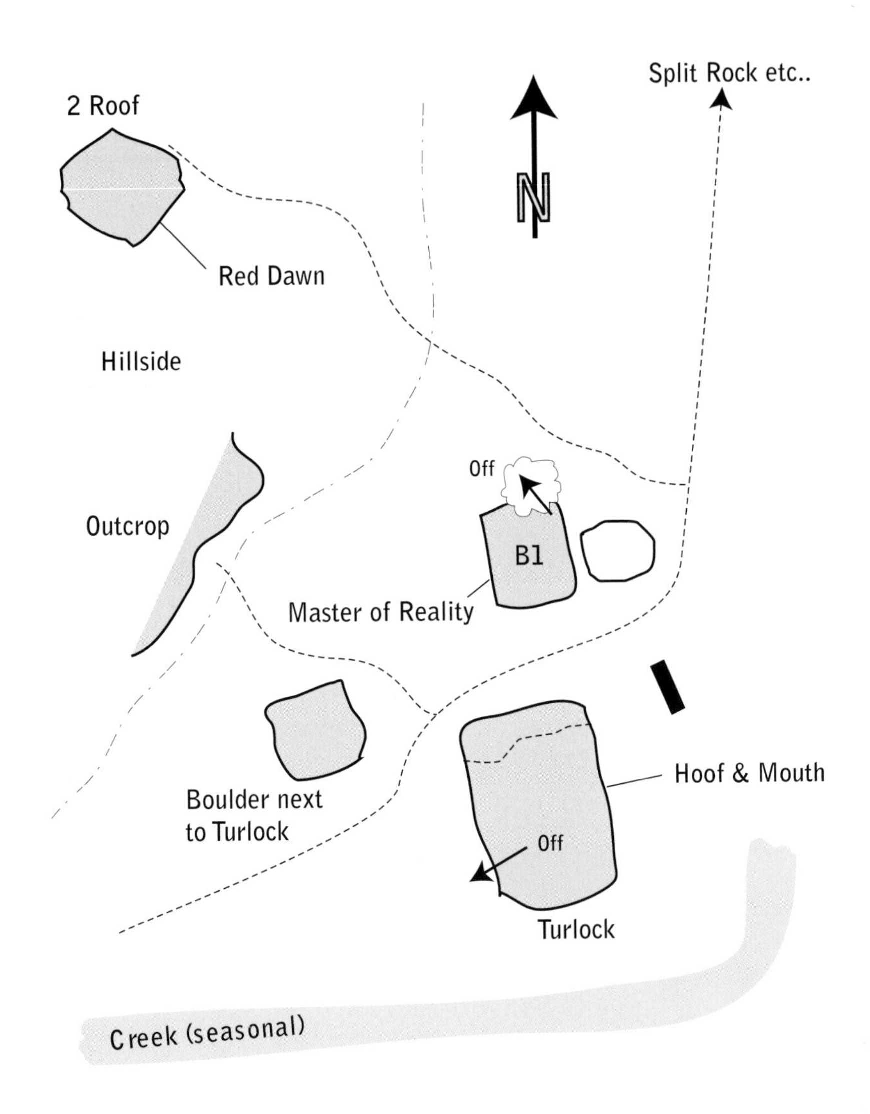

TURLOCK AREA

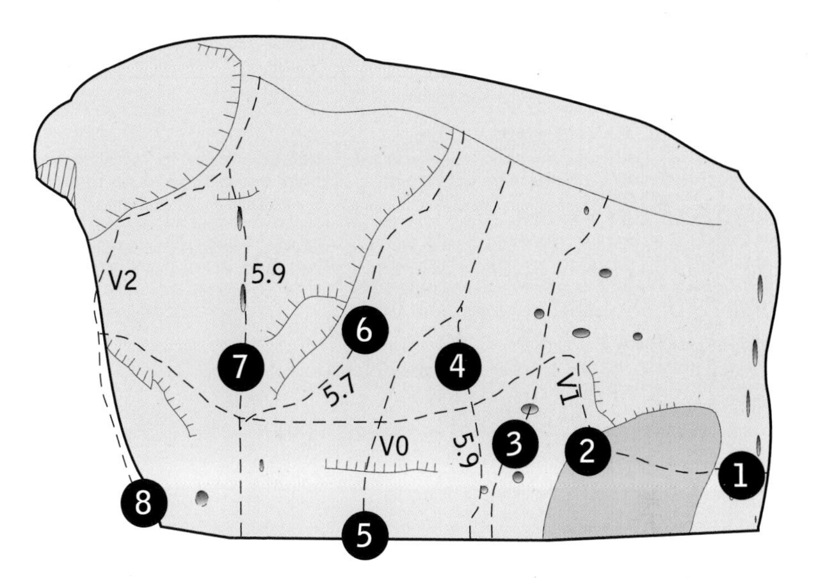

Turlock (aka Boulder 2)

This boulder is very popular with beginners and experts alike, justly so, there are some good routes. The classic back overhanging face and the harder problems are usually bouldered. The bolt anchors on top can be reached by climbing The Stairs. The corridor between Turlock and B1 Boulder probably has the best concentration of moderate to hard boulder problems at Stoney Point.

The routes are described starting at The Stairs and going around clockwise. Route length 25′.

Front Face

1. TURLOCK TRAVERSE★★ V6
Clockwise, from any given point. Three of the corners are hard, the back face and the crystal ball section are hard, traverse from Potholes to Untold Story is also hard.

2. THE BULGE★ V1
Start on the right then using a good pocket, power left, step high; hey this is okay....whoops! A variation **ROCK AROUND THE CLOCK★★** (V1) bears right to join Untold Story, then down and around again, or go counterclockwise. Or just bear right and up the slab just left of Untold Story (nice).

3. THE STAIRS★ VB
An easy beginners route using carved holds. Also the way off.

4. TURLOCK FACE★ V0
A delicate climb on small holds and smears.

5. TURLOCK ELIMINATE★ V0
A tricky mantle leads to smearing. Ignore the big holds and pockets.

6. THE FLAKE★★★ VB (5.7)
Lieback the flake, a tricky move leads over the top. The flake used to be bigger.

7. PIN SCARS (AKA SILENT RUNNING)★ V0
Follow the pin scars, a tough move up and left leads to a depression.

8. THE CORNER★ V2
Lock off on an undercling and, using the arete, head up and left to finish in the crack. Strenuous. **SIT START VARIATION** is rumored to be V10.

North & Back Faces

Some classic boulder problems here, with lots of eliminates.

1. CRYSTAL BALL MANTLE★★★ V5R
Jump or long reach to the ball, squirm up onto it using body English, flakes lead to the committing heel hook move over the roof...left arete to the top of the ball used to be known as Crowd Pleaser but...

2. CROWD PLEASER★★★ V2R
AKA Yabo Roof. An absolute classic with gym like moves up to the crux. Cruise up the left edge, commit right to flakes then prepare for the moment of truth and committing moves up and around onto the face (crux). **CROWD TEASER** (V0) swings left around the arete from the first big jug, and Michael Reardon's **CROWD PUKER** (V5) continues all the way up the arete.

3. NORTH FLAKE★★★ VB (5.7)
The start is the crux, from the ledge step right and head up the flake in a wonderful position.

4. NORTH FACE★ VB (5.7)
The same start as the previous route, but from the ledge head straight up -- a little tougher.

5. FACE ELIMINATE★ V0
The face to the left of Route 3, then joining it higher up.

6. HOOF AND MOUTH★★★ V1
The old yellow book gave it 5.8! Scrunch yourself up in the pocket, a little more; that's it. Now go up and left then across for the good jug.

7. NOSE DIVE★ V6R
Exit right from Hoof & Mouth using a long reach -- high ball.

8. WAUGH PROBLEM★★ V7
Between Hoof & Mouth and Pliers, straight to two dismal slopers, then hand rail. **SLIME VARIATION** (V10) hits the slopers from the left.

9. SLIME★★ V1
Power yields results on this little V1 testpiece, the crux is snatching for the vertical rail from below. Many, many eliminates in this area (at last count 107!).

10. PLIERS★★ V1
Power also yields results on this little V1 testpiece, the crux is snatching for the vertical rail from the left (a tad harder than Slime).

11. THE REAL CRYSTAL BALL MANTLE★★ V6
Opening moves of "Pliers" then work your way left (big crossover with right hand) and slap up and over the sloper. Go for the mantle - no cheating by exiting right to the jugs!

12. RAMADA★★ V0R
After a few bouldery moves a committing lunge for the flake arrives, then cruise to the top. Erosion has created a rather nasty landing. A fun problem if using attentive spotters.

Turlock Pothole Face

A nice place in this area for new climbers to hang out and top rope, then watch the show in the Turlock/B1 Corridor.

13. POTHOLES★ VB (5.6)
There are a few variations to this. The crux is usually getting over the top.

14. POINT BLANK V?
Literally. A broken hold has filed this in the last great problem folder.

15. UNTOLD STORY★★★ VB
A great little route, your first highball. The face left of Potholes is awkward to start and scary to finish.

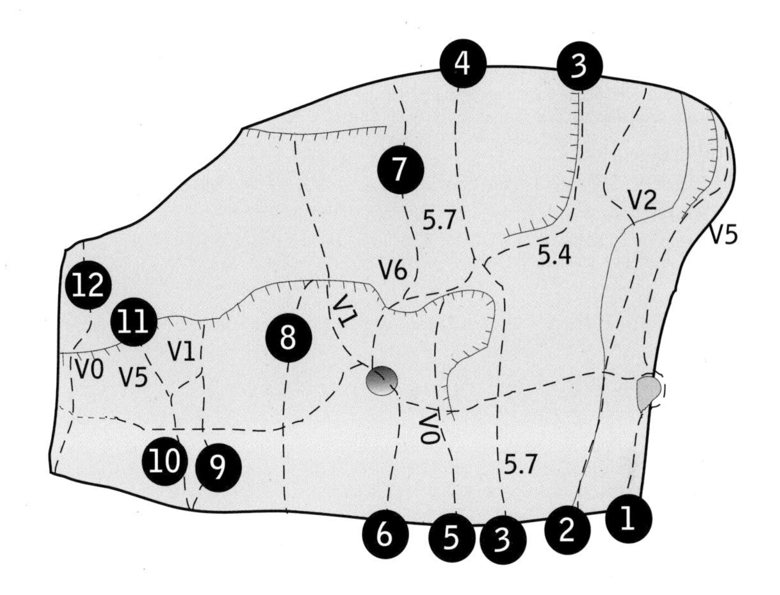

NORTH & BACK FACES

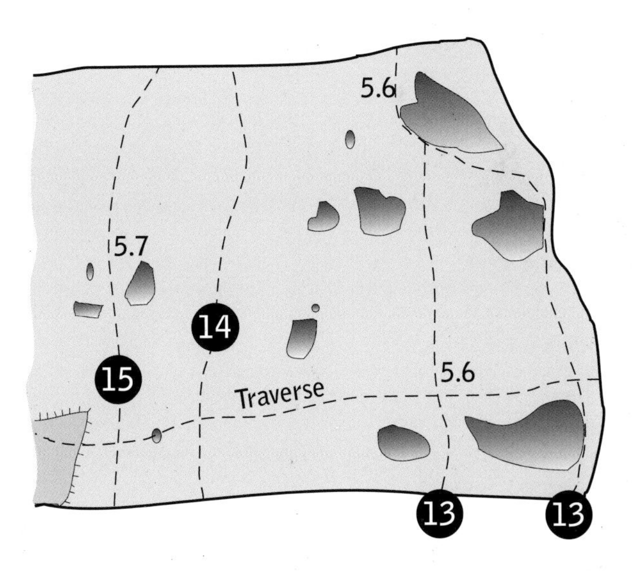

POTHOLE FACE

B1 Boulder

The south face was referred to as "Pink Floyd" in the old yellow book. One of Stoney's best boulders, with som thing for everyone starting at V0 to beyond the fringe. Use the tree at the back to gain terra firma and high five I've tried to distinguish the major lines, once again lots of variations. The routes get harder and harder every year thanks to people pulling the holds off.

1. THE CORNER★★ V0
A super little problem, the 2nd easiest way to the top, good holds and nice moves.

2. ED'S TRAVERSE★★★ V10
Start at the corner and head into "The Ear", then further right and head up finishing on The Crack. Lots of nice positions and moves.

3. HOG TIED★★ V1R
Good flakes lead the unwary to a very creepy crux. Highball, use a top rope, or crash pad and attentive spotters.

4. HOG TIED TRAVERSE V4
Start on Hog Tied and traverse left to finish on The Corner.

5. MASTER OF REALITY★★★ V5
Zen and the art of bouldering. Flexibility and technique lead to a good sidepull, the finish involves committing crimps and smears then stem to the bleak finishing hand match....An easier and inferior variation use to hit the undercling from the left, but erosion has made this inferior version much harder.

6. EXPANSION CHAMBER★★★ V7
Good starting holds just left of The Ear lead to a smearfest top out.

7. THE EAR★★ V6
Somehow get over the bulge to a recess (no more nice little undercut) and wonder why you ever came, top out on slopers.

8. GU aka INSIDE OUT★★ V7
Sit start then slopers and crimps on the right of the recess.

9. PINK FLOYD★ V4
Cheatstone, or pad stack pullup, campus to hold above: mantle onto it. A **WAUGH VARIATION★★** (V10) comes in low from beneath, using small holds. **UDDER PINK★** (V10) finishes here after starting on Rout (11).

10. APESMA★★★ V6
Nice and powerful. Standing start using a right pocket, power up to rail, power up again, then mantle up. C from Route (11) sit start: V8.

11. TITTY F^^K★★ V7
Sit start. Assume the position followed by tenuous power moves rightward towards the top of the crack. Or as a variation up bulge left of Route (12) at V10.

12. THE CRACK★★★ V3/V5
A power problem which does yield to finesse, the crack direct is V5, or dyno for the great slot on the right, V3, or sit start, or undercling, many variations, all great stuff.

13. FLYING CIRCUS★★ V5
Sidepulls and a snatch, then another snatch to a pocket in the face on the right, slap for the top edge.

14. ELIMINATION PROBLEM★ V10
Use the monos to the left of Two Scoops, bad landing on the rock behind.

15. TWO SCOOPS★ V1
Up the edge then left using two sloping namesakes, then squeeze under the tree, uneven landing (roots etc..

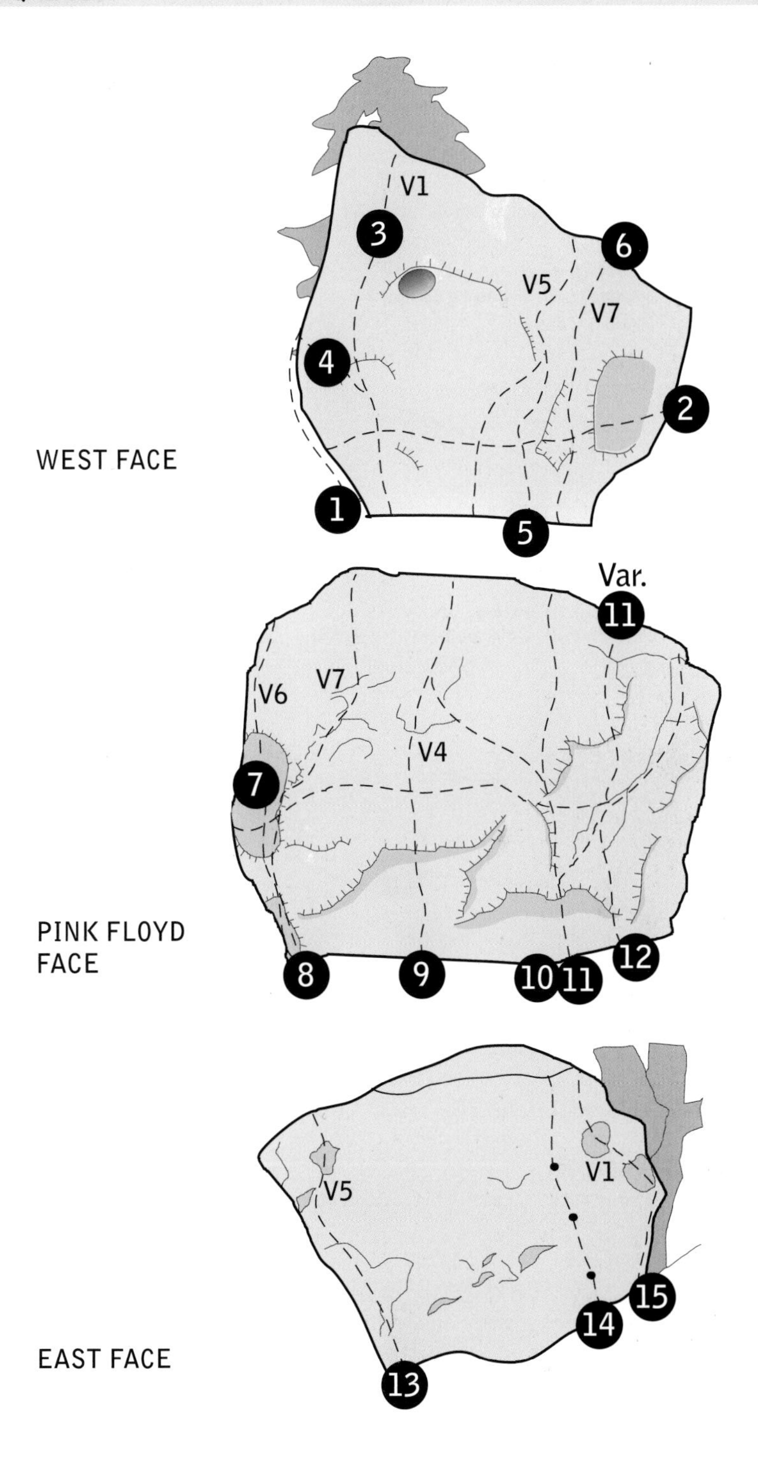

WEST FACE

PINK FLOYD FACE

EAST FACE

Boulder next to Turlock

A couple of fun problems on the north side of this popular spectator hangout.

❶ TRAVERSE★ V4
From left to right, starts out okay, followed by slopers and body tension to avoid touching the rock behind shorties's revenge.

❷ CORNER MANTLE★ V5
Sit start, overhanging to sloping mantle finish.

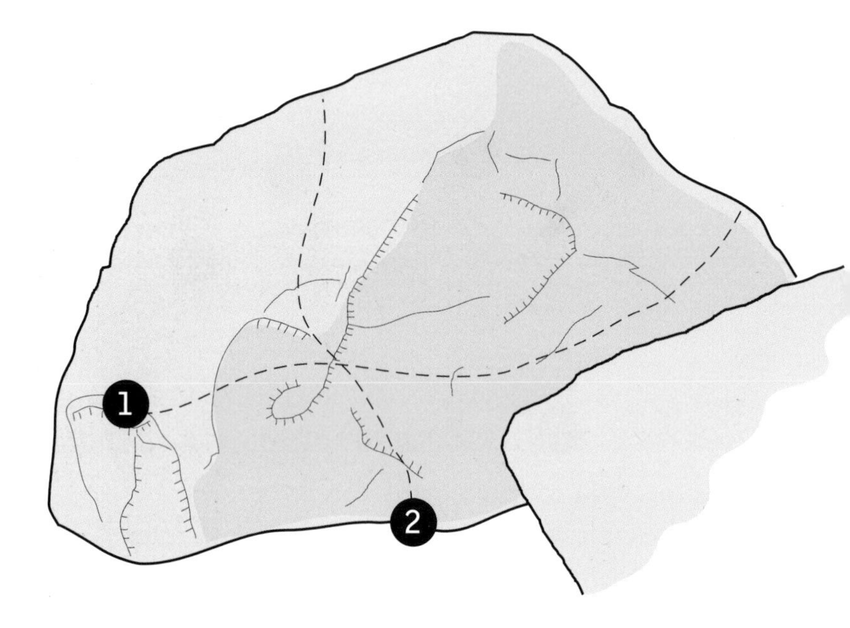

Outcrop

FACE★ V0
(See Page 44). Highball face climbing up the center of the outcrop just up the hill.

Two Roof Rock

This other outcrop above Turlock has a TR. It has two roofs with a rib separating them. Use a thread belay at the back of the outcrop. Route length 35′.

RED DAWN5.9+ ★
(See Page 44). Climbs up the rib between the roofs. The crux is at the top. Take care with the loose holds in the middle.

eastside boulders

Michael Reardon reaching through on Power Glide V6 (Page 62)

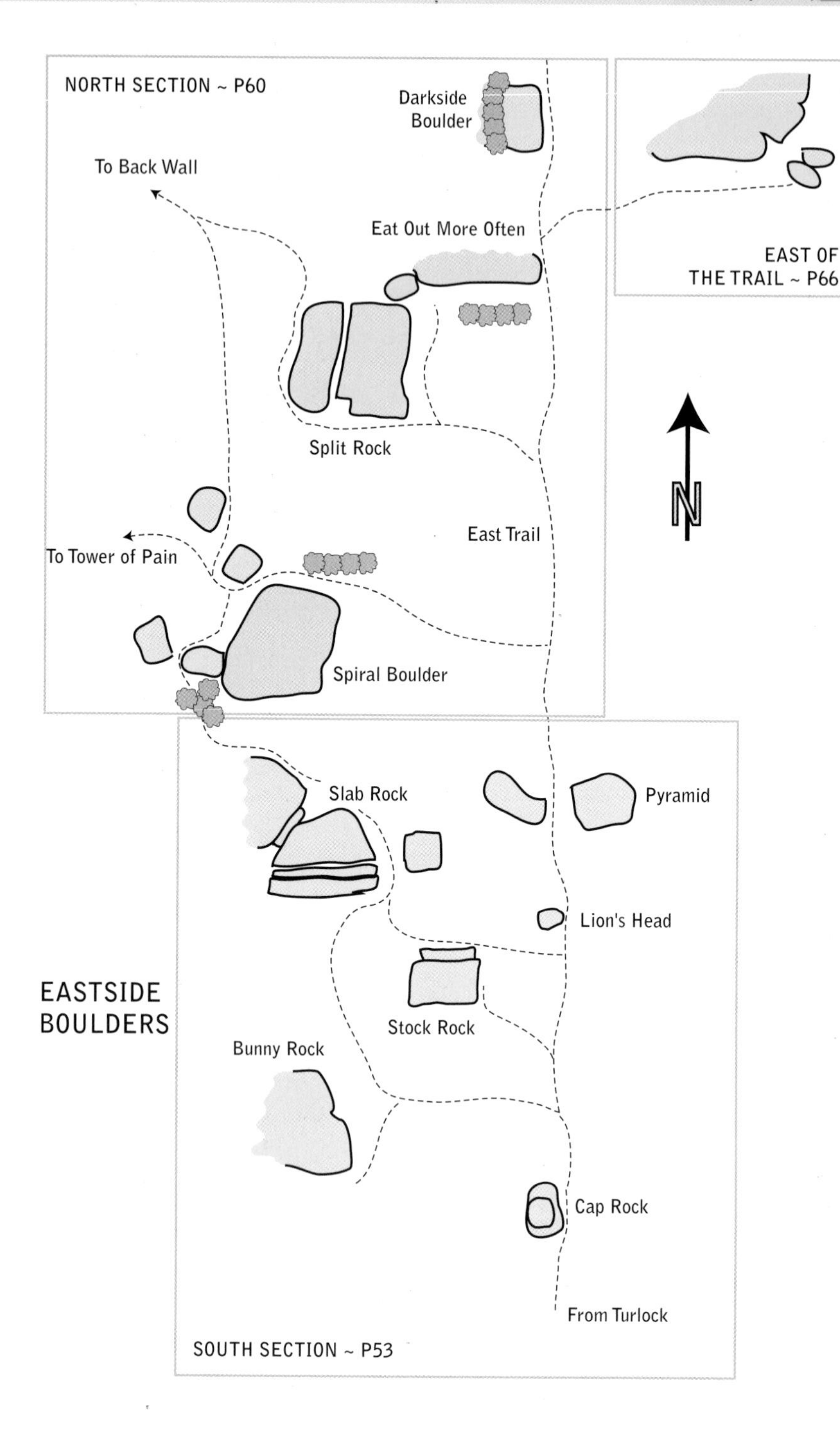
NORTH SECTION ~ P60
Darkside
Boulder
To Back Wall
Eat Out More Often
EAST OF
THE TRAIL ~ P66
Split Rock
N
East Trail
To Tower of Pain
Spiral Boulder
Slab Rock
Pyramid
Lion's Head
EASTSIDE
BOULDERS
Stock Rock
Bunny Rock
Cap Rock
From Turlock
SOUTH SECTION ~ P53

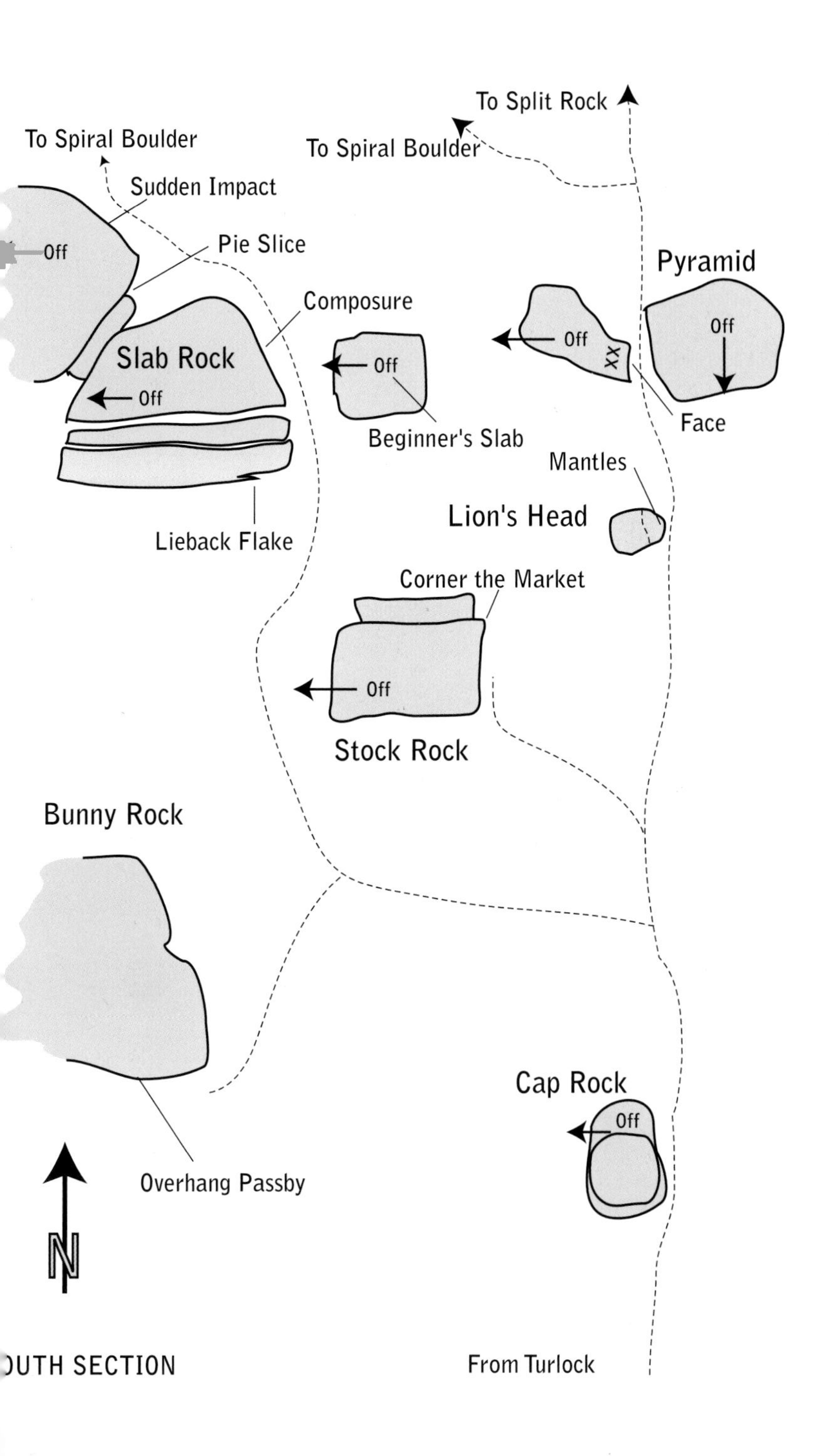
To Split Rock
To Spiral Boulder
To Spiral Boulder
Sudden Impact
Off
Pie Slice
Pyramid
Composure
Off
Off
Slab Rock
Off
xx
Off
Off
Face
Beginner's Slab
Mantles
Lion's Head
Lieback Flake
Corner the Market
Off
Stock Rock
Bunny Rock
Cap Rock
Off
Overhang Passby
N
From Turlock

)UTH SECTION

Cap Rock

Just down the trail from Turlock, on the left, a nice contrast to the overhanging sickness; the fine old art of thi face. Route length 15′.

1 FACE V2
Steep face, sidepulls and mono then pull to crimps.

2 FACE★ V2
Trend rightward, big pocket and sidepull, shoot for sloper, then good hold below the cap.

3 FACE★★ V0
Crimpers to sloper, good foot, then slot under cap.

4 FACE★ V3
Not so good feet, slopers to cap.

5 FACE★ V4
Two crimpers, tiny feet, slap and shoot for top of cap.

6 MANTLE PROBLEM★★ V1
Good left sidepull to sloping mantle.

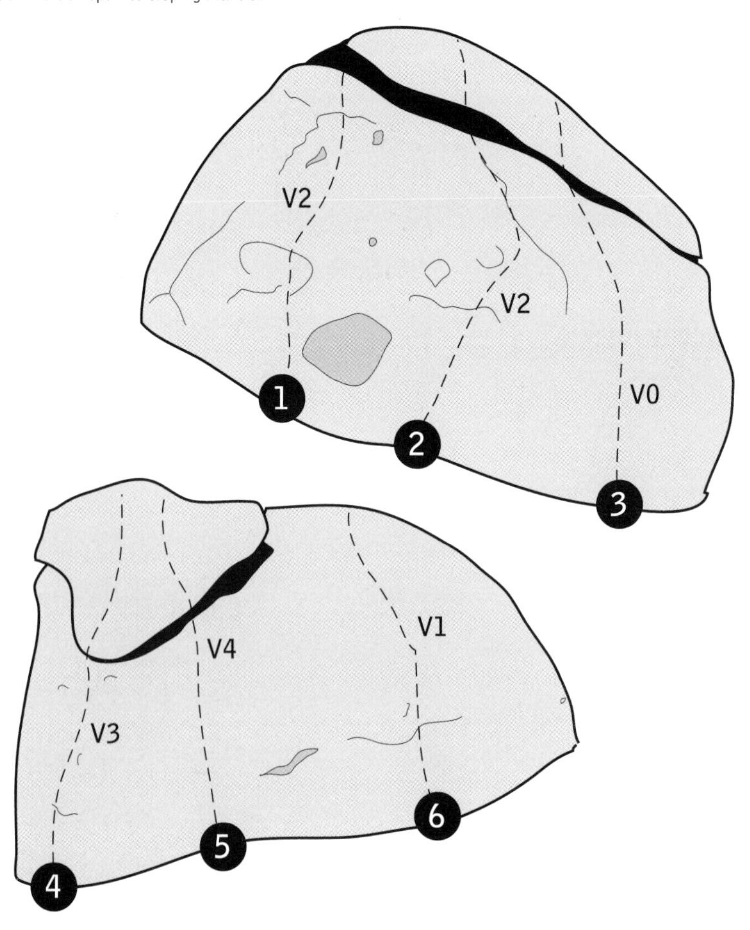

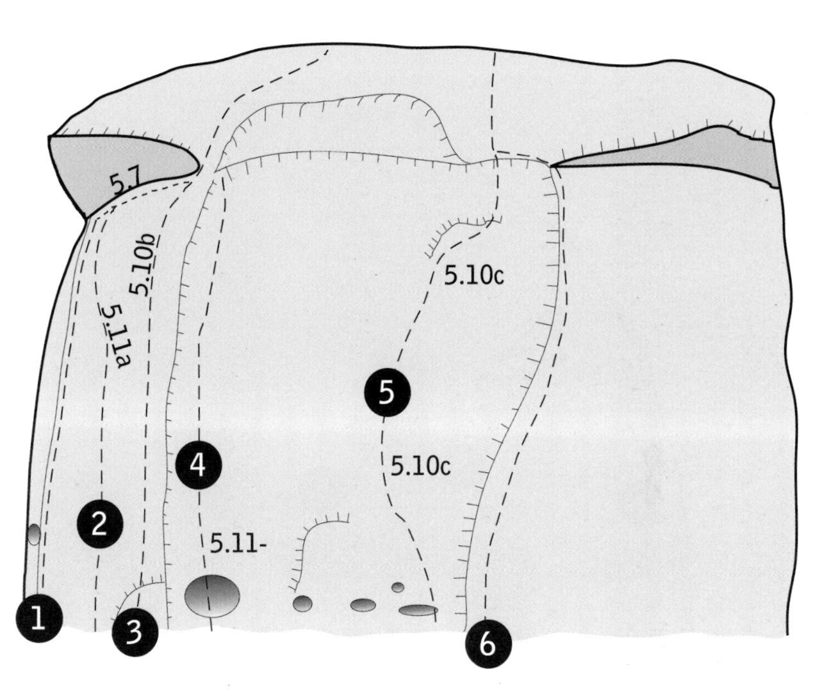

unny Rock

large outcrop to the left of the trail with an unsavory looking chimney on its right-hand side. Sling and cam e boulder on top. Route length 35′.

OVERHANG PASSBY★ 5.7
Follow the crack to the roof then traverse right; crux, follow another crack to the top.

LAYED OFF★ 5.11a
Thin moves lead to a sloping flake, lay off this to reach a hold way left.

OVERLORD★ 5.10b
Pull over the undercut and follow the wall to a long reach; crux, and then the top.

MIDDLE ROUTE 5.11-
Tough climbing up the edge. Hard start.

RABBIT'S FOOT★ 5.10c
Climb the overhanging wall just to the left of the chimney. The start is the crux.

RABBIT'S BUTT ?.??
The must do flaring chimney. Enjoy!

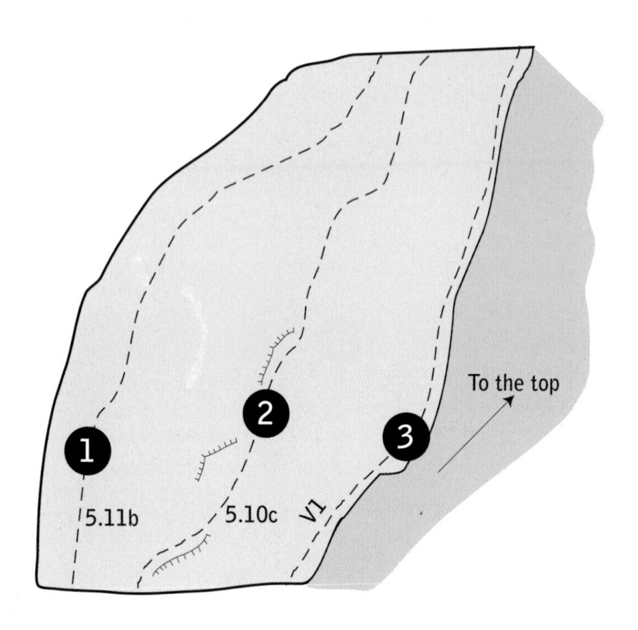

Stock Rock

This boulder sits on the slope, just above and to the left of the trail, before reaching Lions Head. The easiest wa up is on the back which is not that easy. Because of the delicate nature of the holds, I recommend top-roping (although Route 3 may be okay), use a thread belay at the back of the boulder, there are also two 1/4" bolt studs on top. Take hangers. Treat the holds with tender loving care! Route length 30".

EASY MONEY VB (5.9)
On the south side of the boulder. Climb up past a large pocket.

BLACK MONDAY★ V3 (5.11+)
On the south side of the boulder. The blank wall.

❶ BLACK FRIDAY★ V2 (5.11b)
Another very fingery climb just to the left of Bull Market.

❷ BULL MARKET★ V0 (5.10c)
A difficult start leads to delicate edging.

❸ CORNER THE MARKET★★ V1 (5.11a)
Lieback tenuously up the arete, using the boulder on the right to step up reduces the grade to V0.

ion's Head

the left beyond Stock Rock, with a particularly feline aspect.
ere's more than one way to...get over this cats nose, to the left (the eye) and right is easier than trying to antle directly over, which proves to be quite troublesome. V5 direct, V0 to the left and right.

'yramid Rock

the right of the trail, a little further along from The Lion's Head. The south slab is fun for kids. Very sadly this ulder has recently (2008) been brought to its knees by some very offensive chopped holds.

FACE V0
Undercling to left sidepull, hand match on rail.

BULGE V1
Seam (good holds) high step and shoot for big finishing jugs.

SLAB I★ V1
Pocket for feet, crimps then smearing to the top.

SLAB II★★ V0
Easy feet to mono...then straight up.

BODY GERMAN★ V1
Tricky mantle start.

EAST FACE V1 - V3
Fun problem out of the creek with variations.

FACE OPPOSITE PYRAMID★ V0
(See Page 53). Undercut then steep, with scary top out. Two bolts on top if you want to top-rope.

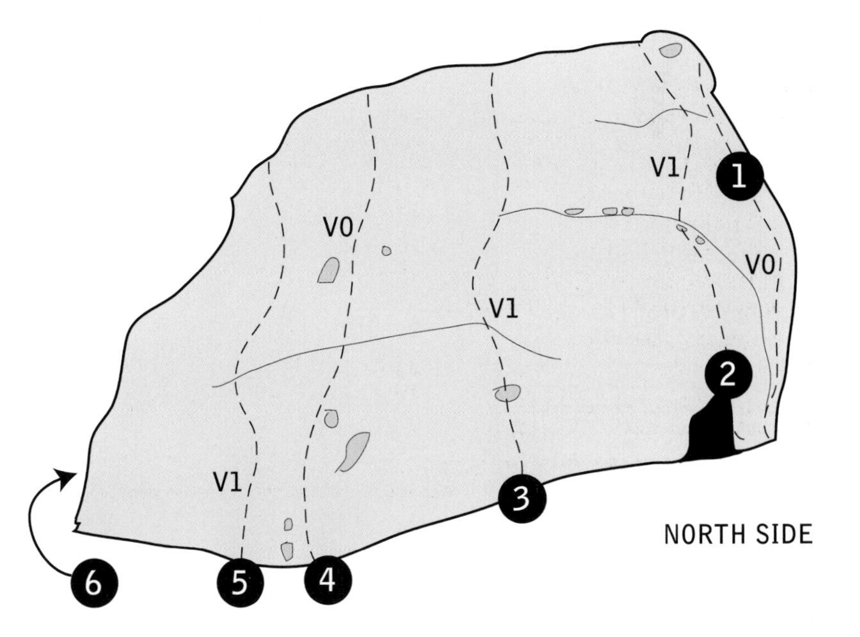

Slab Rock

A large slab just north of Stock Rock, with a fun lieback flake on it's south face. Boulders and cracks on the tc supply adequate anchors if you're top-roping.

1 UP PROBLEM★ V2
The holds start out okay but soon diminish.

2 LIEBACK FLAKE★★ VB
Boldly lieback up the flake. Pity it's not longer.

3 SUGAR POPS V1
A finger wearing series of moves on small pockets, pebbles and flakes. Can be connected with the Ant Line (10) traverse.

4 MEAT GRINDER MANTLE★ V0
Use the ball to 'hop' onto the ledge, easy slab to top.

5 LEFT SLAB ROUTE★ VB (5.6)
Pull up onto the slab and climb the edge.

6 THE SLAB★★ VB (5.6)
Same start as (5) but head straight up the slab - fun.

7 SMEDGE★★ V0 (5.10a)
A tricky mantle leads to very good thin smedging.

8 COMPOSURE★★★ VB (5.9)
Another mantle start leads to moves which must be exact or else (especially if you're high ball bouldering!).

9 THE SLIDE★ VB (5.8)
After rounding the corner climb up the edge.

10 ANT LINE★★ V0
A traverse from right to left, balancy and unique for Stoney.

PIE SLICE V0
(See Page 53). Fist crack or lieback.

SUDDEN IMPACT★★ V6
(See Page 53). The mother of all Stoney pin scars is located up the slope on the right of The Slab. Read it and weep. Tiny, but kind of positive pin scars.

BEGINNER'S SLAB VB
(See Page 53). Another slab down and east of the above slab is a nice place to practice easy Class 5.0 slab technique. A few ways to go.

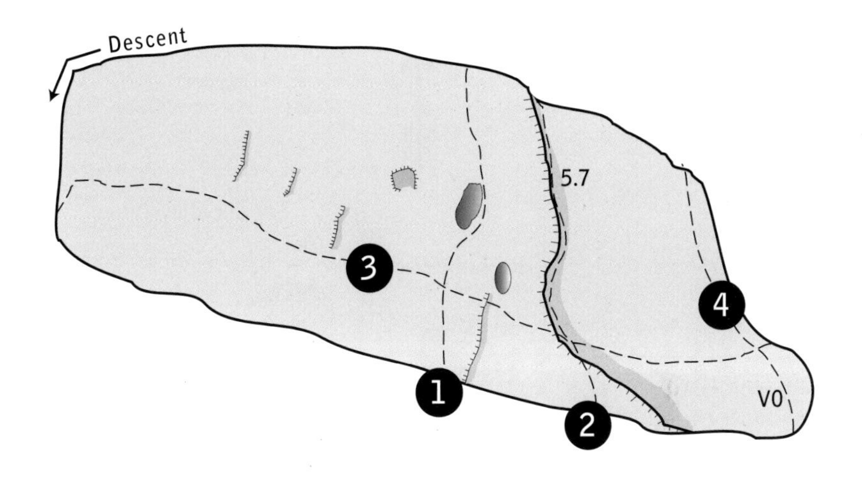

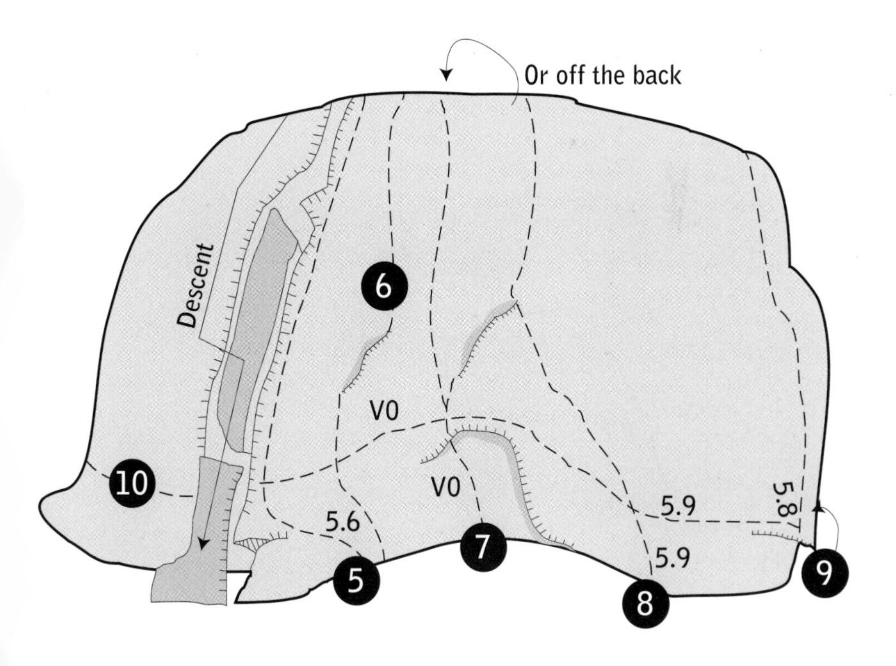

ike Martin cruises the Lieback Flake VB

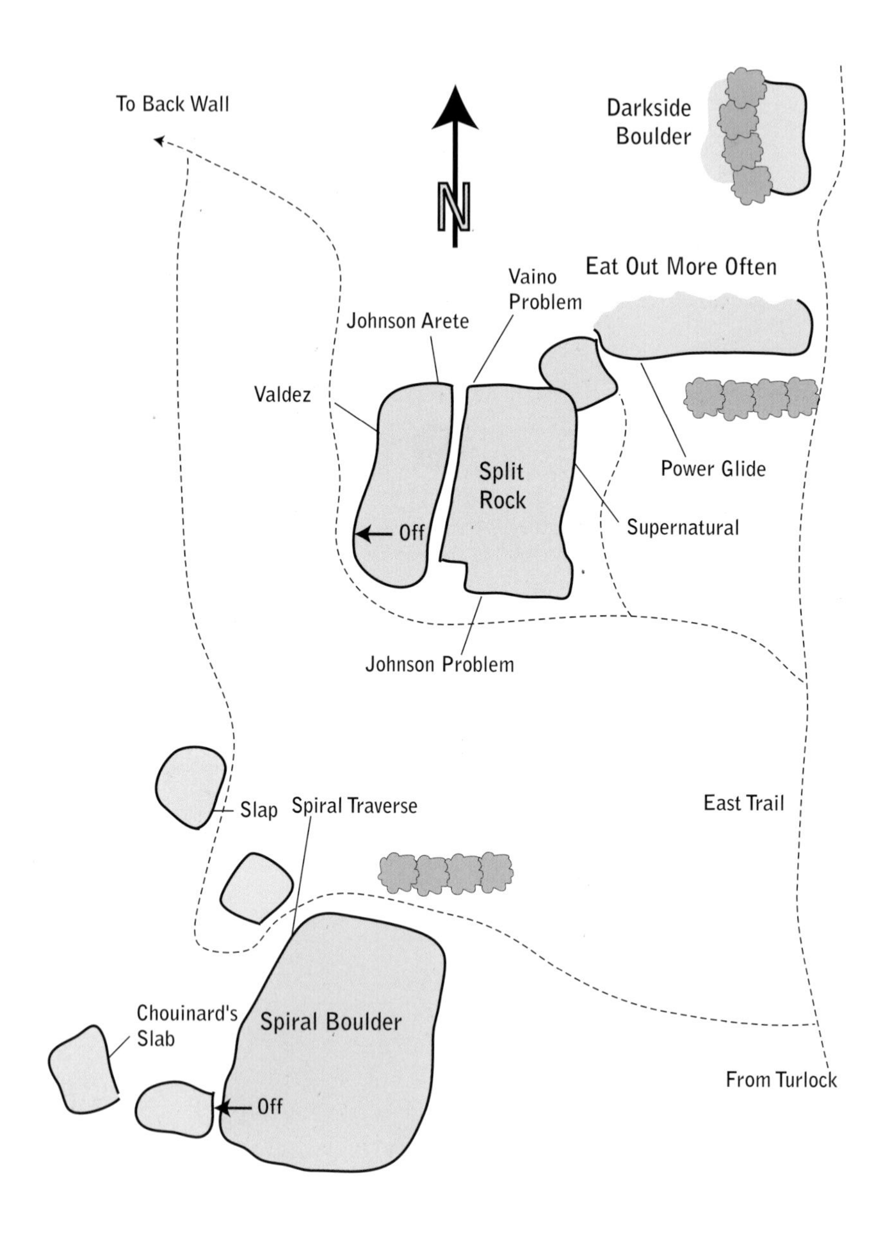

NORTH SECTION

piral Boulder

nis is the massive boulder on the left just before reaching Split Rock (cut left at hitching post). Cracks at the ottom of the boulder on the south side provide the anchor. Route length 35′.

BOLDDURING★ V0R (5.10a)
Jump for a flake and follow it to a gravel filled depression. Foot pedal to the top.

BOREALIS★ V0R (5.9+)
Climb up side pulls then a face. The delicate slab leads to the top.

SPIRAL TRAVERSE★★★ V1
This is a classic boulder traverse, generally it goes from left to right and is very fingery. Start way low with a lieback flake. It's changed over the years, so leave well alone when wet.

SPIRAL LOW TRAVERSE★★★ V2
Like Spiral Traverse but stay low and head for a good pocket, then up; a little trickier.

SPIRAL DIRECT★ V0
Up to the undercling, then a faith move to the pocket above.

SPIRAL DIRECT II V0
Up where Spiral Low goes up, finish on mossy rock.

CHOUINARD'S SLAB★ VB
(See Page 60). A thin smearing problem straight up the slab.

SLAP★ V1
(See Page 60). A short boulder problem that is deceptively hard when there is no chalk to define the right holds.

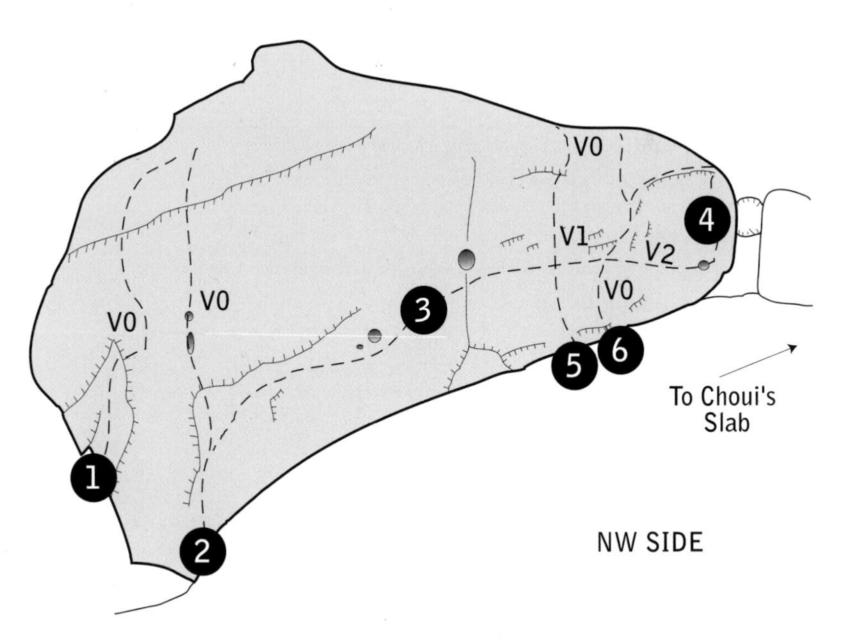

Split Rock

This formation is cleft by a large chimney, which is recommended as practice for chimneying. There are some righteous boulder problems here too. For an easy way to the top, climb up the short west face; take slings and nuts if you need an anchor. Route length 35′.

1. JOHNSON PROBLEM★★★ V7
Vertical rail to hand match in pocket. A very big move (physically and mentally) to hold on the lip... welcome to the Johnson Problem.

2. SPLIT DECISION★★★ V1R
A bouldery start leads to an overhanging corner with a crack for thin fingers.

3. THE CHIMNEY★★ VB
Squeeze up into the depths of the chimney; tricky. Then using the classical method head to the top.

4. ARETE SKELETON V0 (5.10c)
The overhanging arete to the left. (Top rope).

VALDEZ★ V1
(See Page 60). Ball to sidepull, then edge to sharp jugs and finish.

JOHNSON ARETE★★ V8
(See Page 60). The right arete (of chimney), slopers and leg hooks on the edge.

VAINO PROBLEM★ V6
(See Page 60). The left arete (of chimney), trending left on slopers.

SUPERNATURAL★ V4R
(See Page 60). Steep face to crux move onto slab, follow to top.

Eat Out More Often

Some great tough boulder problems here, including a withering traverse.

5. EAT OUT MORE OFTEN★★ V3
Traverse right starting just left of Power Glide. The seam as far as it goes.

6. POWER GLIDE★★★ V6
Pulling ability pays dividends...undercling to slopers/edge, throw for slot, finish directly.

7. STANDARD ROUTE★★ V2
Seam, then pockets to crimper. Feet. Then shoot for good finishing hold.

8. TREE ROUTE★ V3
Crimpers to pocket then seam, another pocket to grainy top out..

9. MOSAIC THUMP★ V9
Sit start, campus up to hand match on seam, traverse off, yet to see top out.

DYNAMIC DUO V3
Face on the end of the formation, parallel to the East Trail.

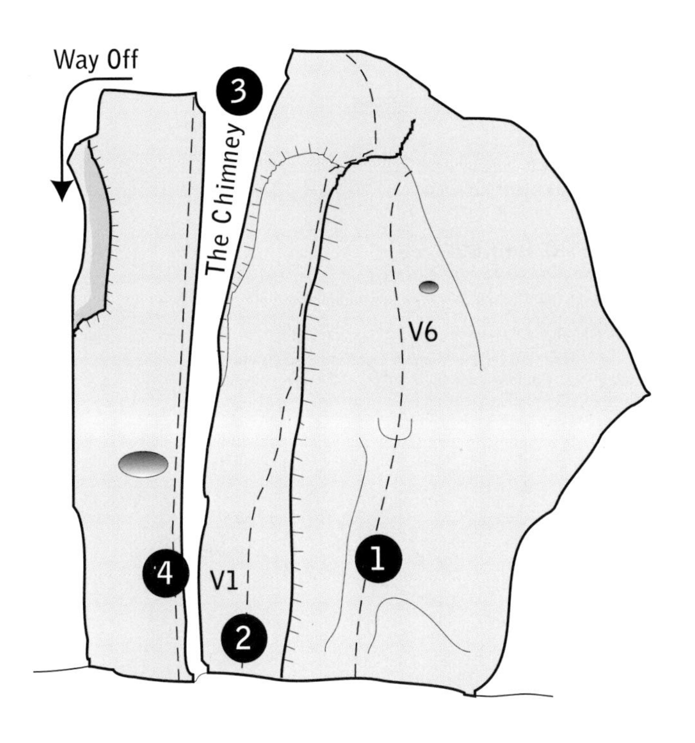
Way Off
3
The Chimney
V6
4
V1
2
1

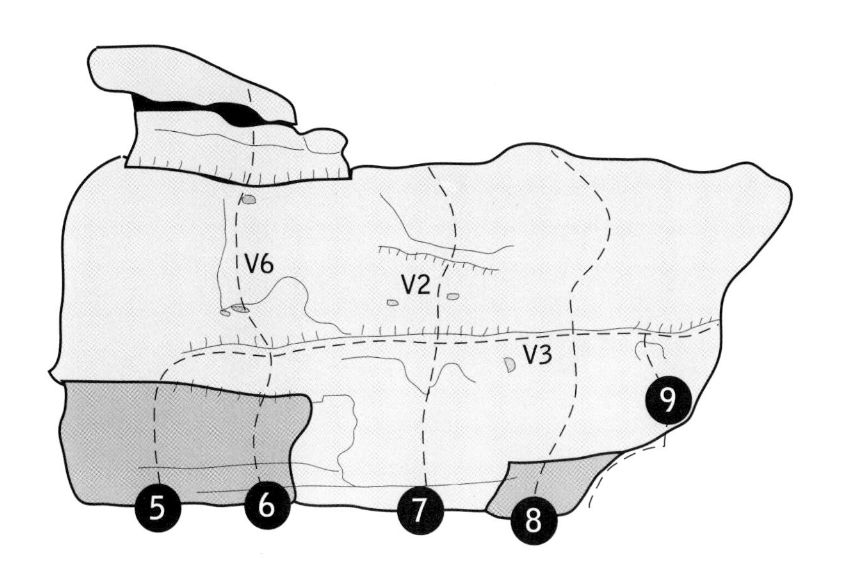
V6
V2
V3
9
5
6
7
8

Darkside Boulder

Just past the Powerglide Area, left of the trail in the bushes. Top out, descend right using the branches, spot on the descent would be nice.

❶ DARK SIDE OF THE RAINBOW V1
Left sidepull and right pocket enable (with the right foot correctly placed) a lunge for a good flat hold high up, match hands then mantle using the grainy/slopey top.

❷ BLACK AND BLUE V2
Left sidepull, right sloper, a knee bar enables shorties to grab small crimp. Good holds on the arete to iffy topout. Tall people can dispense with the kneebar and reach right for the small crimp V0.

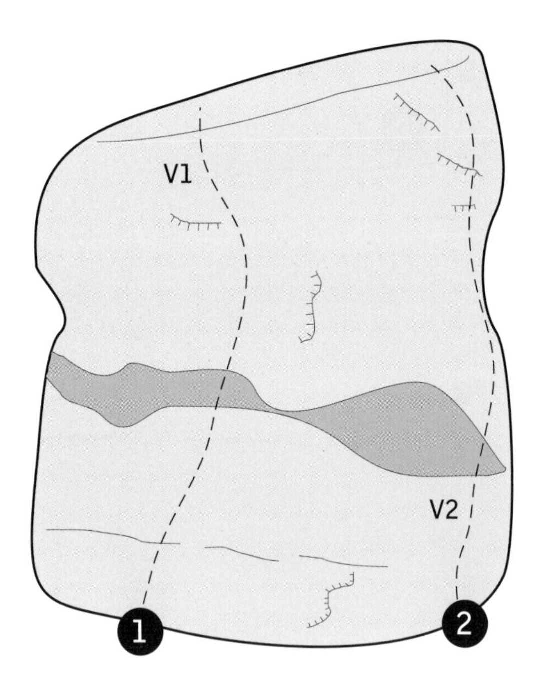

'ower of Pain

his is the large pointed boulder up on the side of the hill above Spiral Boulder. There a couple of fun climbs on . Thread a small chockstone at the back for an anchor. Take a hanger, there is also a bolt on top. Be careful, iere are some loose holds. Route length 35′.

1 PREYING MANTIS★ 5.10b
Steep climbing on good holds leads to a delicate crux, follow better holds over the top.

2 MANTIS MANTLE 5.11a
Climb straight up between the other two routes, very thin.

3 CAPTAIN ENERGY★ 5.11a
More good steep climbing to a difficult step right using a hidden pocket. Resting at the ledge proves to be a pump, so head straight up on doubtful holds.

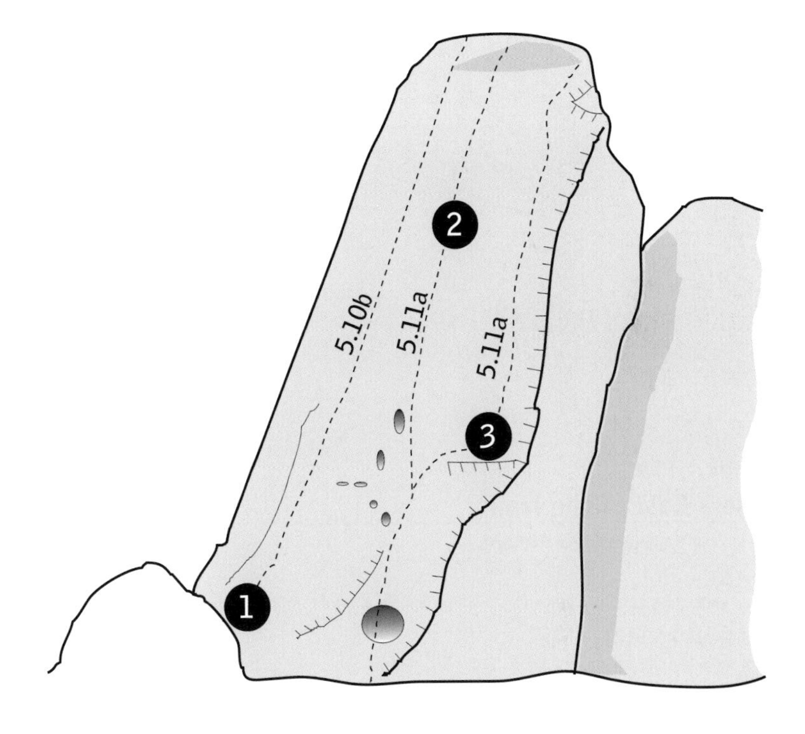

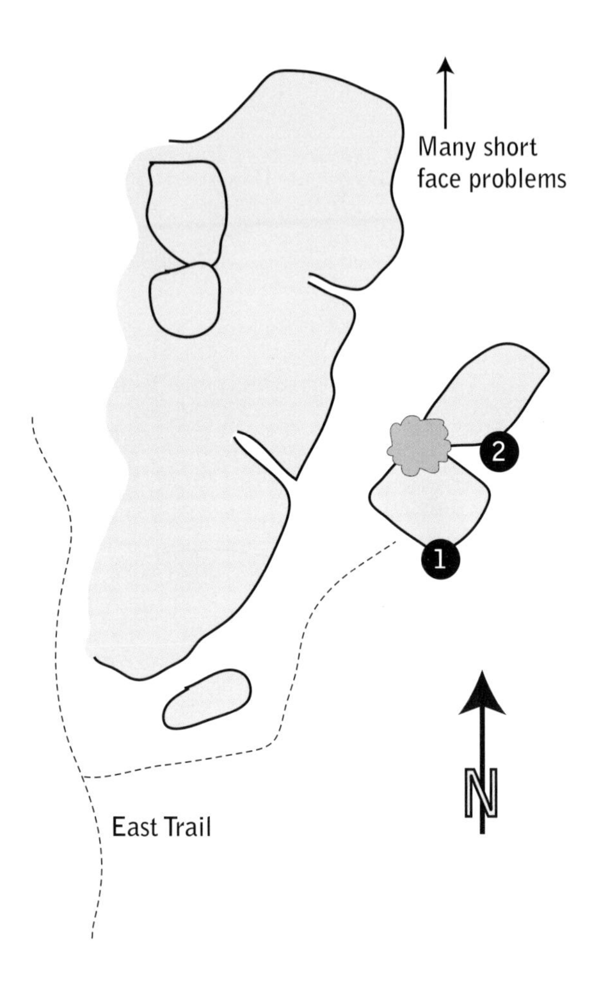

Boulders East of the Trail

Surprisingly not a huge amount of stuff here.

1 BULGE★ V0
Huge undercling to hidden jug.

2 CAVE V4
Overhanging arete on sloping side pulls to horn. Big pull over the top. Tree is now covering the finishing moves.

back wall

A cool Chris Savage on A-Frame Right 5.9 (Page 69)

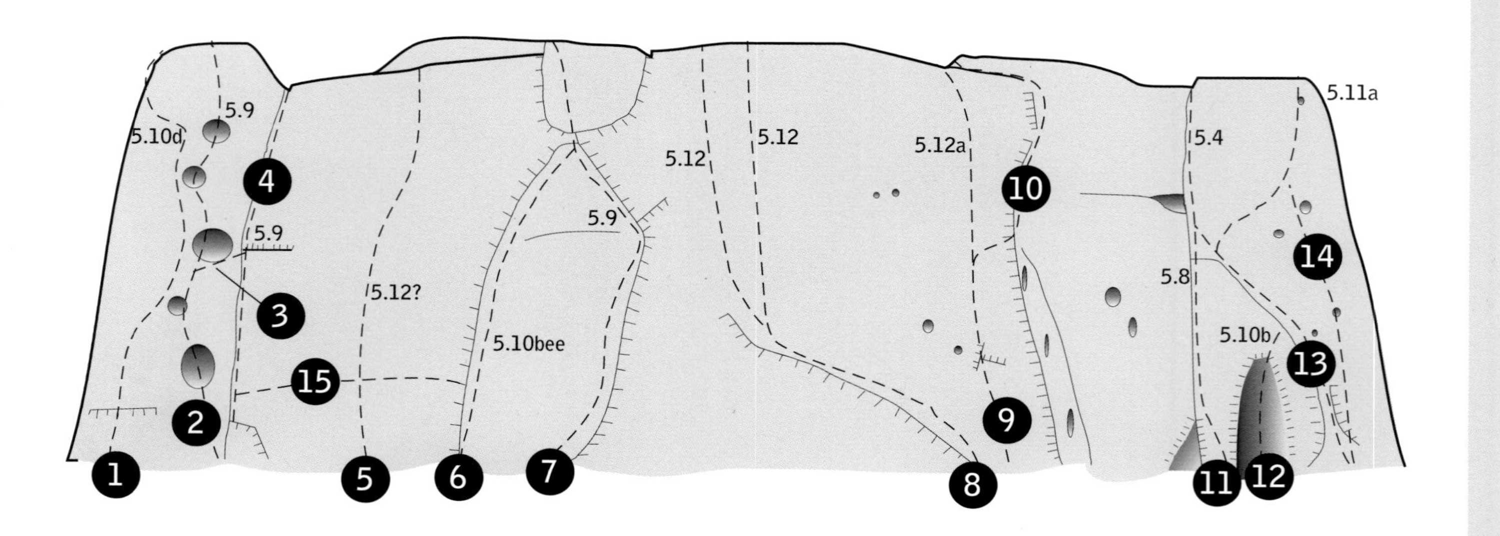
5.10d
5.9
4
5.9
3
2
1
15
5.12?
5
5.10bee
6
5.9
7
5.12
5.12
5.12a
10
9
8
5.4
5.8
5.10b/
11
12
13
14
5.11a

BACK WALL

The Back Wall

There's some very steep climbing on this wall, all good stuff, even a couple of moderate routes. Gain the top from either a gully to the left or go up past Beethoven's. The anchors are slung boulders and nut/cam placements; Vicious has a two bolt anchor on top. Route length 35'/40'.

1. THE WRATH OF KAHAN★ 5.10d
Climb the buttress to the left of Potholes. Some good moves.

2. POTHOLES★★ 5.9
Swing from hole to hole then make a tough move over the bulge. Squirm over the top.

3. POTHOLES ESCAPE★★ 5.7
Follow the potholes, but before reaching the bulge make a committing traverse right into the crack. Thrutch to the top.

4. POTHOLES CRACK★ 5.9
Jam the crack over the overlap. Can be led.

5. DART LADY 5.12
A Waugh creation, follow very small holds over the bulge. Recent information suggests that holds may be missing.

6. A-FRAME LEFT (AKA TARZAN) 5.10b
Awkward jams and sandy rock make this most strenuous.

7. A-FRAME RIGHT★★★ 5.9
A classic crack in a world of faces. Follow the ramp to the right and pull up to the hanging ledge. The crux is leaving this via a tenuous lieback.

8. THE PLANK 5.12
Up the ramp, then either left or right up the steep wall above. Only bee keepers need apply.

9. VICIOUS★★ 5.12
Potholes and pin scars lead to a lieback to gain the little pocket. A series of small but positive reinforced holds lead to another pocket. Bouldering moves sometimes lead to the top.

10. OWL HOLE★ 5.10c
Mortals can head right from the pocket and go up over bulging rock. Finish up the pin scarred corner.

JAM CRACK★ V0
Left of the following route. Good practice, no top out.

CHIMNEY 5.7
Just left of Route 11. Most nasty, but entertaining, no top out.

11. BLACK'S CRACK★★ 5.7
An awkward start leads to a strenuous pull onto easier ground. Finish up Beehive.

12. TELEPHONE BOOTH 5.10b
A short but strenuous exercise, the crux is pulling over into Beehive.

13. BEEHIVE★★★ 5.4
Classic easy climbing up a chimney followed by an exposed corner guaranteed to thrill.

14. BEEGONE★ 5.11a
Climb the Beehive chimney then step onto the wall using big holds and potholes. These lead to the right edge. The final pothole allows the top to be reached, the crux is making a very strenuous mantle over the top. Can also be climbed direct starting just left of The Prow.

15. POTHOLES TRAVERSE★★★ V1
From left to right; following the chalked holds proves quite strenuous adding a return, even more so. There's also a low variation and some up eliminates. It's also possible to traverse the entire Back Wall and around onto Beethoven's, a long voyage.

East of the Back Wall

These Boulders in the brush to the east of the Back Wall seem to have fallen out of favor over the years, probably due to the hectic pace of the undergrowth, which now seems to cover everything.

1 ACE'S TRAVERSE★ VB
From right to left, traverse the slab using the lip then pull over, or do an eliminate (harder) without the lip. Good for beginners or kids.

2 FACE V0
Short face problem.

3 FACE V0
Short face problem.

4 THIN FACE V0
Crimpy and smeary.

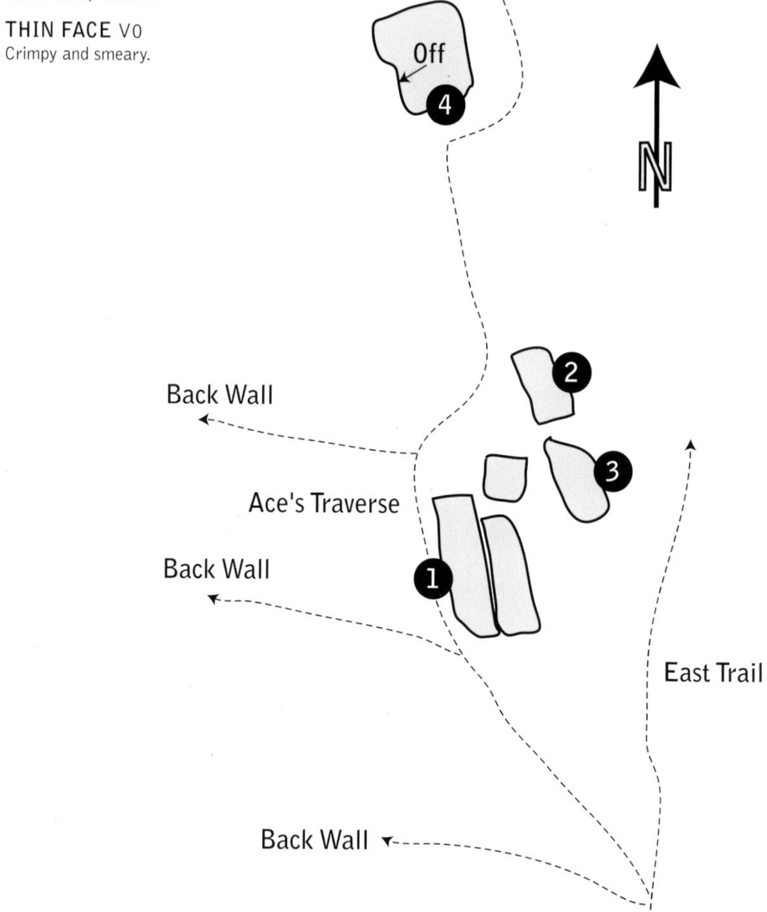

north canyons

Michael Reardon solo on The Prow 5.11a (Page 79)

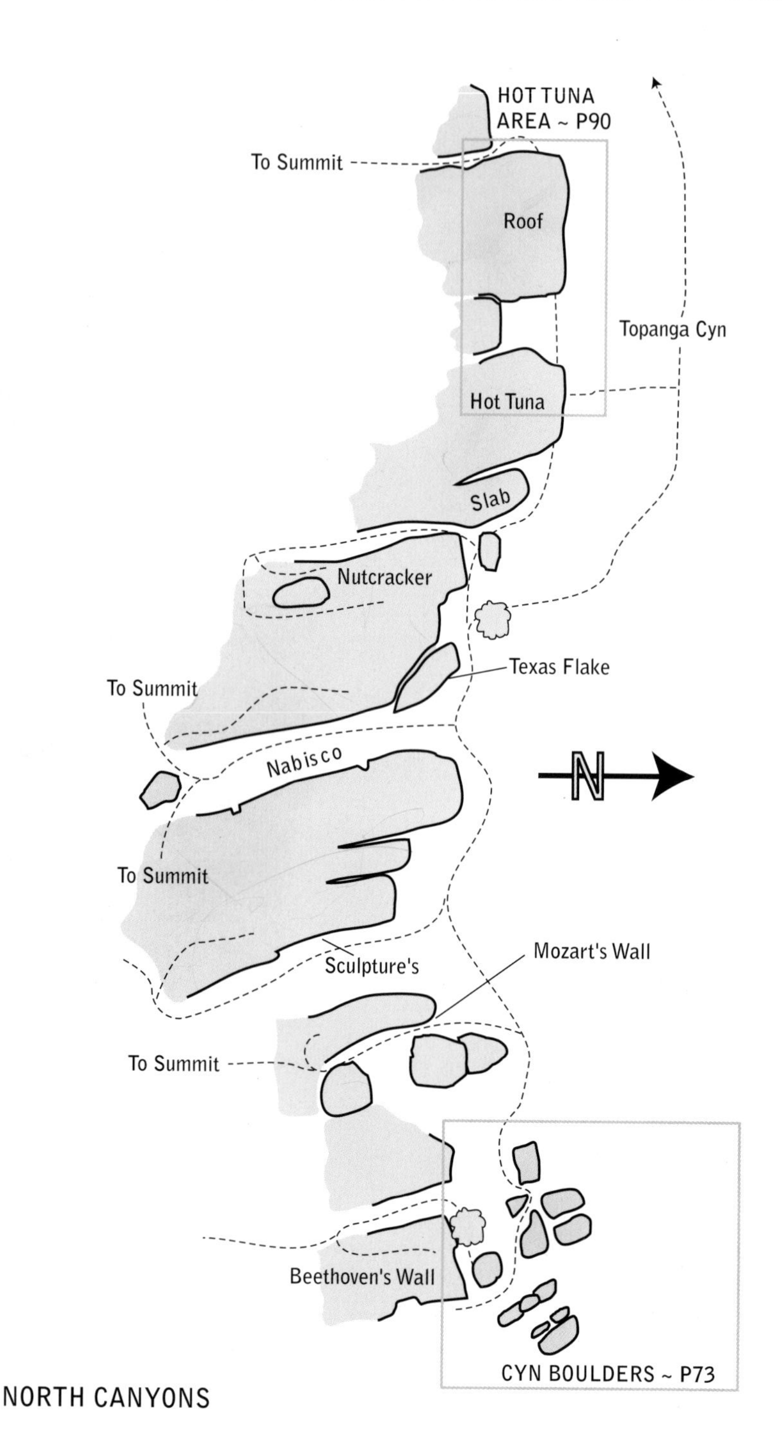

NORTH CANYONS

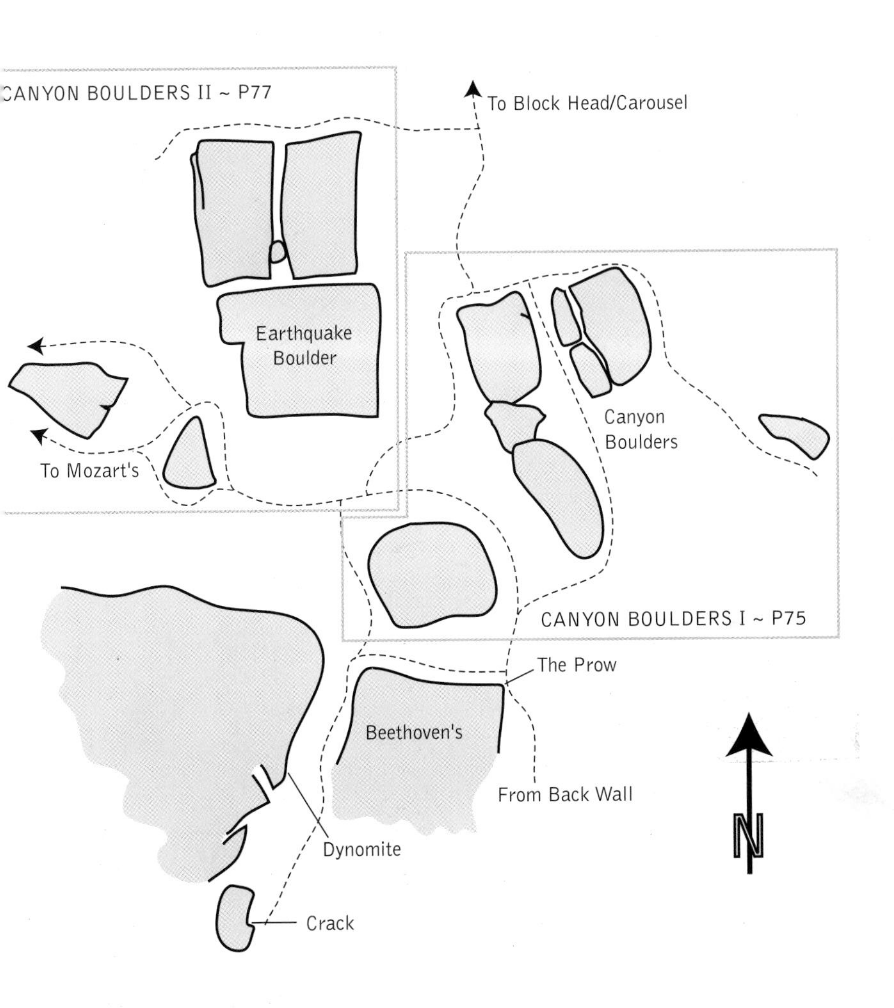

CANYON BOULDERS OVERVIEW

Canyon Boulders

This, the Brickyard of Stoney Point deserves major attention.

1. EASY FACE VB
Easy face on positive holds. Descend down the south side.

2. SHORTY SHEA V0R
Thin start to ledge, undercling to top.

3. SCRAMBLED EGGS TRAVERSE★★★ V3
Steep and sweet to horizontal band, then tricky towards the Bird Hole, finish up this. Easier if you're tall.

4. THE BIRD HOLE★ V1
Reach the hole via a stiff little pull - mantle over, then another.

5. CRACK V0
Wide, then narrow to top.

6. ARETE★ VB
Body English and smear your way up the rounded south arete. Descend down Route (7).

7. EASY FACE★★ VB
A very fun problem on good holds to the tiny summit. Descend the route.

8. FACE VB
Crimpy on flakes.

9. FLAKE TO NOWHERE★★ V2
A compelling line. Lieback flake to sidepull then shoot for good hold up high, better holds to top.

10. KODIAK CORNER V3
Follow the arete all the way.

11. PANCAKE★★ V2
Diagonal crack to strenuous mantle, short but sweet. Sit start is V4

12. FACE★ VB
Nice face on positive holds. As a variation: just left, crimpier and V0.

13. FACE★★ V0
A strangely satisfying route. Up face, tricky, then snatch left to finish on positive holds.

14. ARETE WITH NO NAME★ V0
Up the edge of the arete then swing to the right, mantle and top out just left of the previous route.

15. OZONE FACTOR V1
Iffy flakes. Descend NW side of boulder.

16. CRITTER CRACK★★★ V0
Great little route! Face and ring-jam to crack, then things seem to get serious.

17. MANTLELOBOTOMY★ V1
Ahh jeez...undercling to slopers, then mantle.

18. THE FONT★★★ V7
Sticktion. Use a not so good solution pocket to gain two slopers, mantle/squirm over and onto the slab.

19. SPOOKY★★ V1R
Tricky balancy moves lead to a steepening and squirmy commitment.

20. ARETE★ V4
Come in from the left, aiming for a pocket, slab to top.

21 **MEATHEAD★** V6
Big 2-handed dyno from the undercling.

22 **SCORPION★★** V3
Steep moves lead to a barely in control reach for a crimper, compose, slap for sloper, then mantle over.

23 **OVERHANGING ARETE★** V5
Sloping sidepulls to a grovel over the top, traverse into pocket on the right is V5, or hit the top move by sit start on the left and sloping traverse right up the arete (V4).

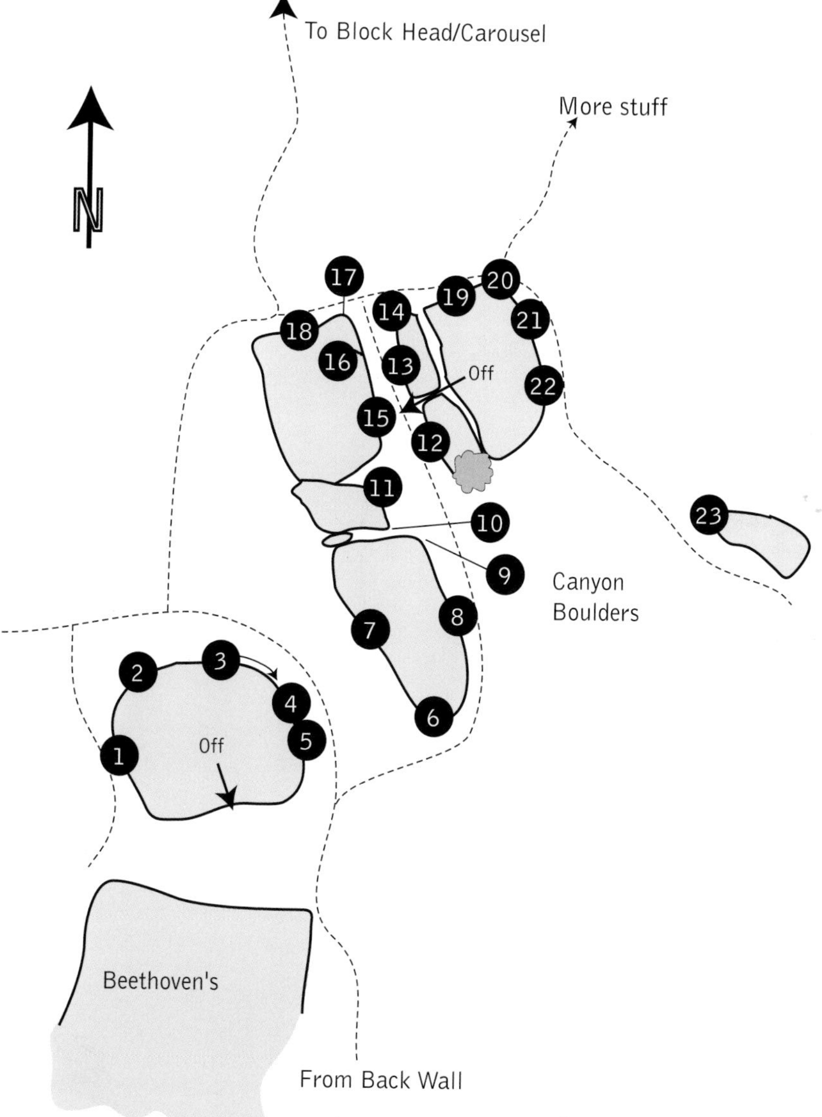

CANYON BOULDERS I

Canyon Boulders continued...

1 EARTHQUAKE PROBLEM★★ V0R
A creation of the Northridge quake, big holds lead to a high crisis: flat holds above a truly nasty landing. ORIGINAL START★ (V0) climb arete on the left, traverse right to hit the flat holds. TR might be a good idea.

2 INCUBUS★★ V6R
Undercling on left seam to pocket in right seam, slap for the top.

3 KODAS CORNER★★★ V3
Holds on the right enable a committing step through while lunging up the rail, take a deep breath and go for it, mantle top out. Direct start V5. A variation climbs the left side of the arete @ V3. There's also a dyno for the mantle top out from the opening holds(!).

4 RIGHT ARETE V2
The face and arete on less than perfect rock.

5 CORRIDOR TRAVERSE★ V1
Rising traverse on right-hand wall on fairly good holds.

6 GUAR SCAR★★ V4R
Crux then pockets to very thin vertical seam.

7 UNNAMED ARETE V3
Palmy with toe-hooks and smears to mantle top out.

8 ARETE VB
The last arete on the right.

9 RAMP V0
Slabby start to juggy wall.

10 ARETE V0
The overhanging arete on good holds.

11 FACE V0
Thin face practice with eliminates up to V0.

12 ARETE V0
Lieback up the rounded arete.

13 ARETE V0
Overhanging arete on sidepulls, shoot to rail, heave up.

14 WINGSPAN★ V3
Sidepulls then slap for the arete.

15 MR-T OF REALITY★★ V4
A Zen problem. Good holds to hand match on small rail, mantle and high reach for top.

Diana Jew is all smiles on Kodas' Corner V3
Michael Reardon Collection

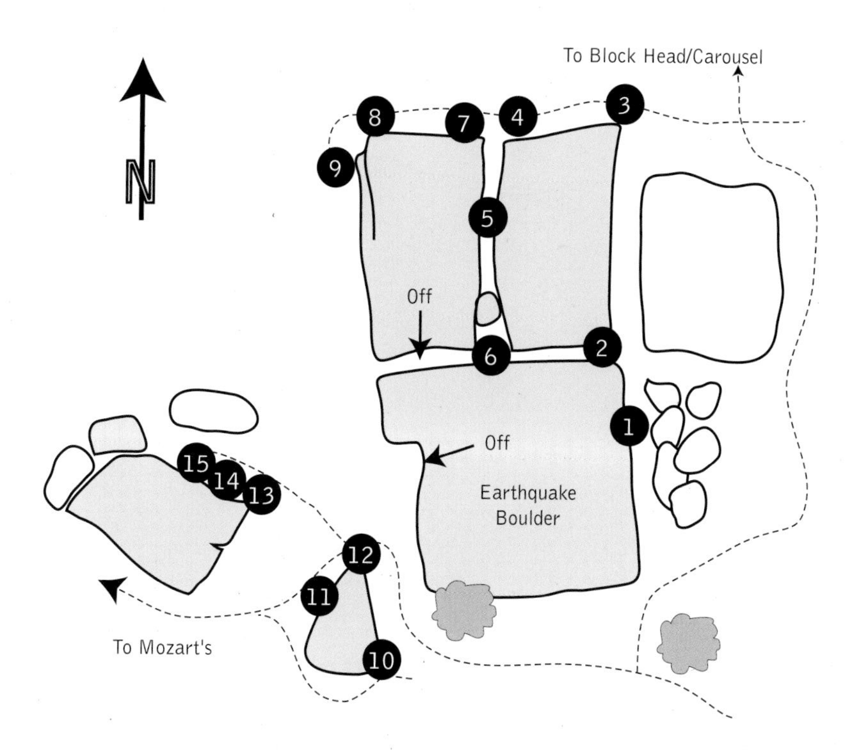

CANYON BOULDERS II

Michael Reardon wills himself to stick on The Font V7 (Page 74) | Michael Reardon Collection

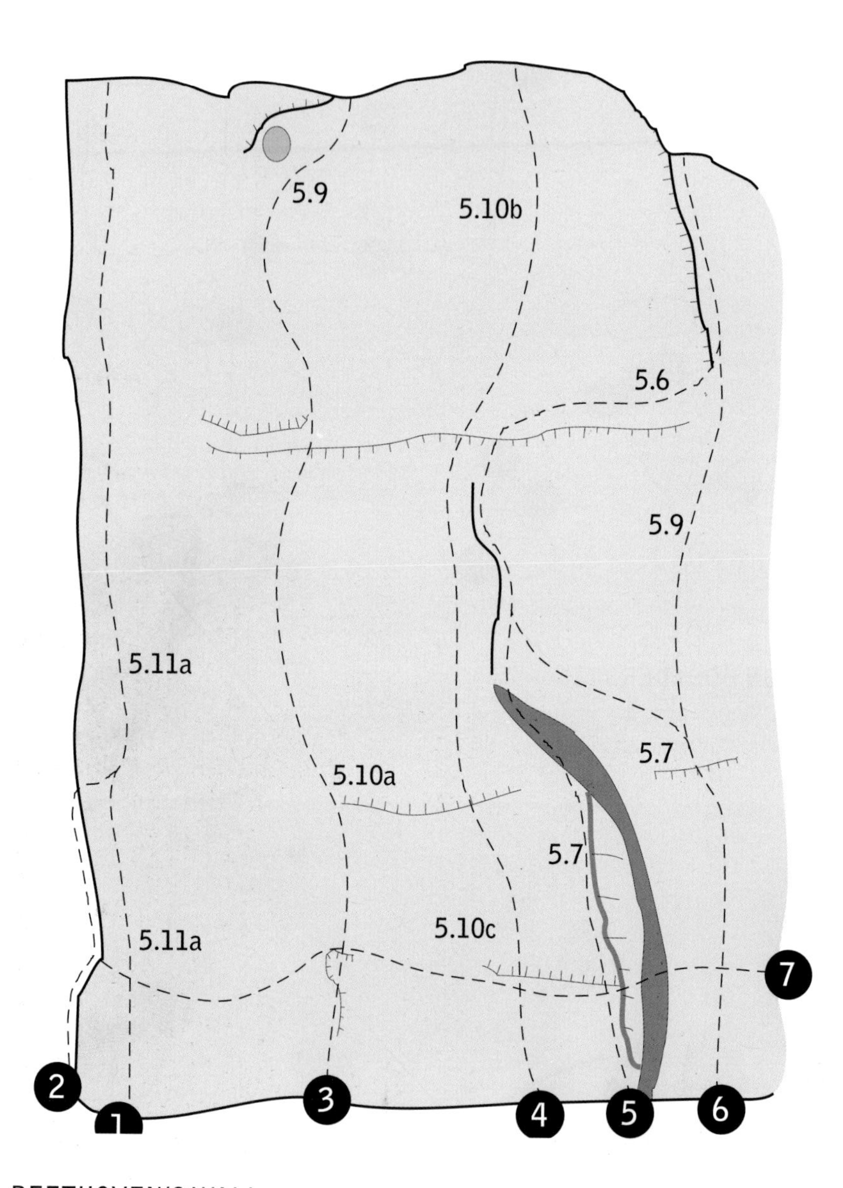

BEETHOVEN'S WALL

Beethoven's Wall

his is the most popular wall at Stoney with good reason, there are some very good face climbs here. Arrive arly to avoid disappointment. The top can be gained by a gully to the right. There are some boulders up there r slings and nuts. Route length 40′.

LEFT EDGE★★ 5.11+
Climb up the edge around to the left of The Prow.

1 THE PROW★★★ 5.11a
A magnificent climb up the left-hand edge of the wall. The first section is very sustained, either up the edge or, slightly harder, up the face to the right. Continue up the edge to the top.

2 VARIATION START TO THE PROW★★ 5.11a
The mid section can be gained by climbing the wall around the corner to the left and swinging around onto the sloping footholds.

3 CENTER ROUTE★★ 5.10a
This line is just to the right of The Prow. The crux is stepping onto a sloping hold about 10′ up, but save some strength for the finish.

4 DIRECT ROUTE★ 5.10c
Climb straight up just to the left of the crack. Hard start and hard finish.

5 BEETHOVEN'S CRACK★★ 5.7
A good moderate climb. Up the crack to the ledge, delicately traverse right and finish up another crack.

6 MANTLE START★★ 5.7
Start to the right of the crack, do a mantle move and join the previous route. It is also possible to climb up the steep wall above the mantle, this is 5.9.

7 BEETHOVEN'S TRAVERSE★ V0
Same start as (2) then heads around the corner and right. Worthwhile if no-one's around.

DYNOMITE★ 5.12
(See Page 73). This climb is located in the approach gully on the right-hand side. A tricky start leads to a lieback flake, up this then make a very strenuous and technical traverse right to a pocket. A couple more moves lead to the top.

CRACK★ V0
(See Page 73). Pinscars to clean crack.

Marc Burns dances up Quickstep V2 (Page 81)

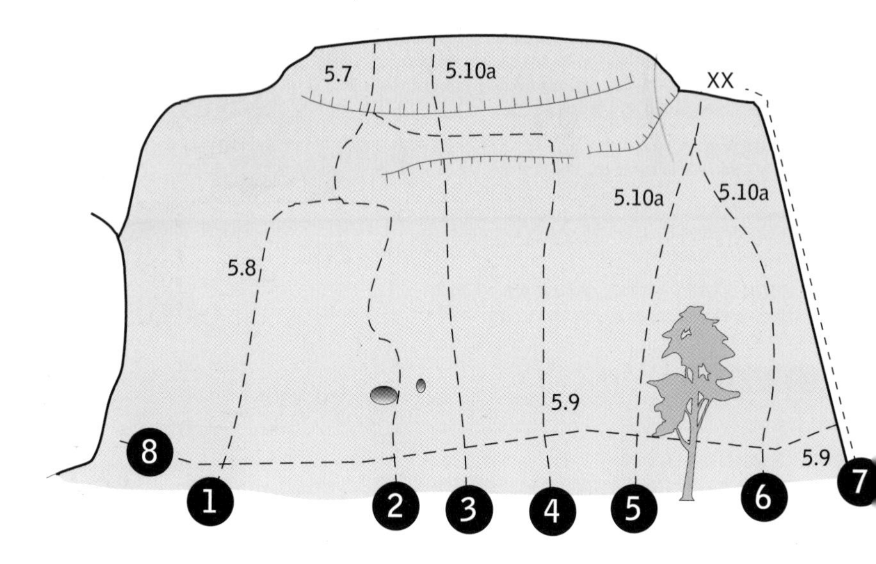

Mozart's Wall

This formation is tucked away in an alcove around from Beethoven's. There are several very good face climbs located here. Access to the top is from either a gully on the far left of the wall or around to the right before reaching the wall itself. There are several bolts on top; so remember to take some hangers, although a boulder could be slung as back up. Route length 40′.

1 FAR LEFT ROUTE★ 5.8
Follow holds to a tricky move before joining the Lefthand Route.

2 LEFTHAND ROUTE★★★ 5.7
A great route with an exciting finish. Start below the big pockets and trend left to the top overhang, a lot c people lower off from here, bogus; because getting over this is the crux.

3 DEAD CENTER★ 5.10a
Climb straight up immediately right of the previous route, make a dyno-mantle over the overhang.

4 CENTER ROUTE★★★ 5.9
A good steep wall climb with a delicate start. The crux is about 10′ up. After that it's good positive holds to finish on the right to avoid the overhang, it is possible to traverse left to join the finish of the Lefthand route.

5 AMADEUS★★ 5.10a
Similar to the Center Route but the holds are smaller.

6 AMADEUS II★★ 5.10a
More face climbing fun close to the right edge.

7 RIGHT EDGE★★ 5.5
This fun slab is good for beginners and very popular with the REI classes.

8 MOZART'S TRAVERSE★★★ V0
Traversing from left to right is a "foot-pump", the crux is turning the corner at the end.

Boulders near Mozart's Wall

1. **ARETE★ V0**
Start off on loose holds, big long jug left of the arete, up to pocket, then top.

2. **MR TOAD'S WILD RIDE★★ VB (5.8+)**
Head up the crack on the west side and over the prow. The crack on the east side leads to the prow also. There is a short route on its east face just to the left of the crack. Use nuts and one bolt stud for the anchor. Or major highball.

3. **FACE V0**
Committing moves up loose flakes.

4. **SEAM STEALER V7**
Left of the SW Edge.

5. **QUICKSTEP★★★ V2**
Dance up the arete using a rail on the left and pin scars on the right, shoot for the big hold and pull over. Very sweet.

6. **SANDLOW PROBLEM★ V6**
A hard pull leads to a tricky finish.

7. **HAND CRACK V1**
Grainy and grovelly.

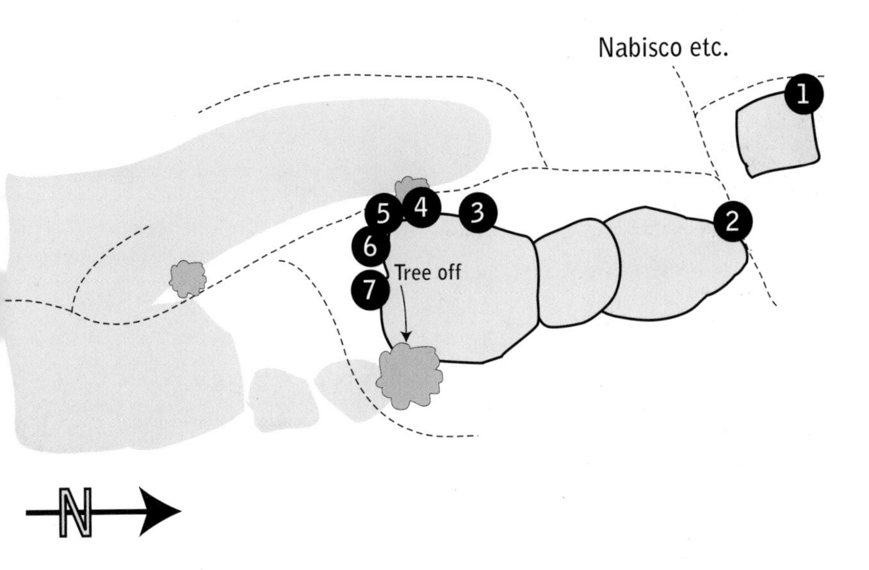

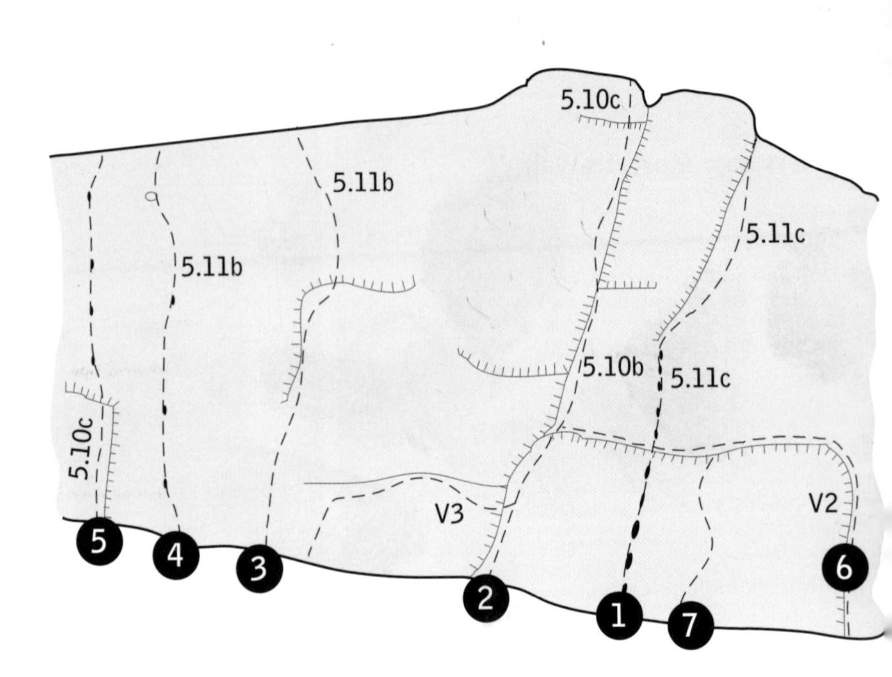

Sculpture's Crack Wall

The routes on this overhanging wall offer very sustained strenuous climbing, mainly in old pin scars, not everyone's idea of positive holds. However the climbs are very good. There are bolt anchors at the top of the first two routes (despite the fact that natural protection is available). The other routes require sling and nut set ups. Route length 30'/40'.

❶ SAND BLAST★ 5.11c
Follow the pin scarred crack over the top; the crux is near the end. At about halfway it's possible to leave the crack and go up the face to the right. This makes it easier, cold comfort for the weak and needy.

❷ SCULPTURE'S CRACK★★★ 5.10c
A 3 star pump! Climb up to the corner and lieback all the way, saving some strength for the crux move over the top, which may turn out to be a belly flop if you're in any way impaired.

❸ CARLSBURG★ 5.11b
Follow an undercling flake to the right, then head straight up on very thin holds; the crux is getting over the top.

❹ SCULPTED CRACK RH★ 5.11b
Technical moves up barely adequate pin scars lead to slightly better holds. Go straight up.

❺ SCULPTED CRACK LH★ 5.10c
A problematical start leads to strenuous pin scars.

❻ SCULPTURE'S TRAVERSE★★★ V3
From right to left. Problematic lieback, then hand traverse, while drowning in a sea of lactic acid, all the way to Sculpture's Crack for a rest...then down and around (crux) to incipient seam.

❼ SCULPTURE'S ELIMINATE★ V5
The face to the handrail of the traverse on tiny holds. SDS goes at V8.

he Walls of Nabisco Canyon

posite the easy climbs of the East Wall lie some of the hardest TRs at Stoney Point. These climbs are very erhanging and require endurance and technique. The anchors used to be the boulders in the gully behind the); climbers are invited to continue to use these, although few can resist the convenience of clipping the bolted chors. Head down to the end of the canyon and go either left or right depending on which wall you wish to set . Route length 30′/40′.

he Outside Wall of Nabisco Canyon

WALL AND SLAB 5.9
This climb lies on the buttress to the left of the East Nabisco Wall. A wall is followed by a low angle slab which steepens towards the top. The anchor for this route consists of nut/cam placements.

QUICKSILVER 5.9+
Steep loose climbing.

MERCURY 5.10a
Up and right to a sandy traverse, then straight up the end of the buttress.

WINGED MESSENGER★ 5.10b
Up the overhangs at the end of the buttress.

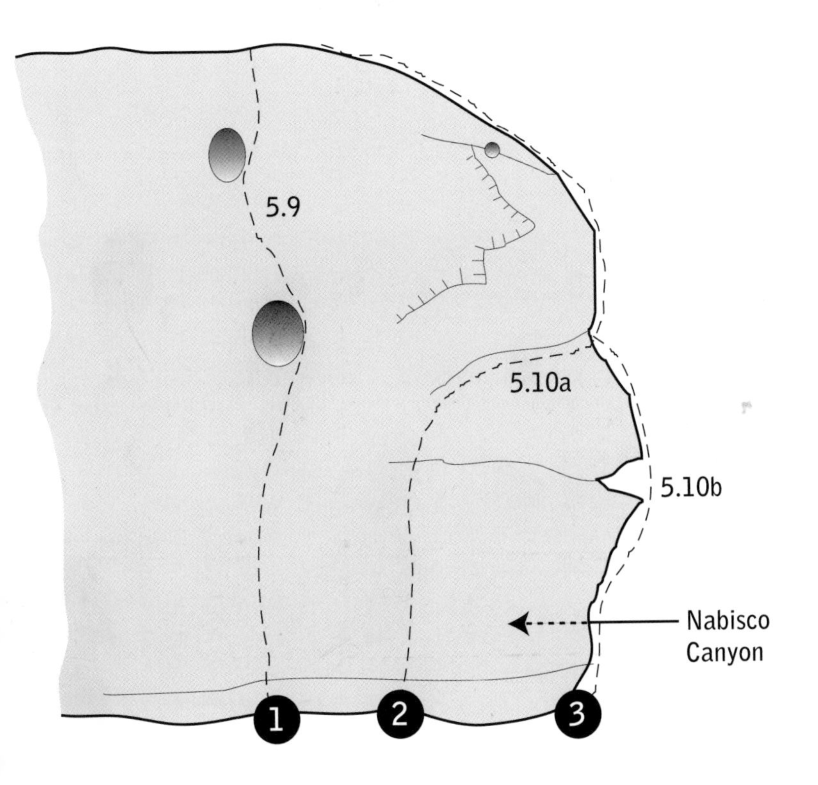

Nabisco Canyon

There are some worthwhile moderate routes located on the East Wall (left as you look into the canyon). Slings and nuts make up the anchor. If you want to get pumped in under 10 minutes, try the West Wall. Don't crank too hard on the holds as some of them are brittle. Treat these climbs with the respect that they deserve.

1. LEFT ROUTE★ 5.9
Climb up the overlaps to the left of the groove.

2. EAST WALL GROOVE★ 5.7
Up the groove and, just before the overhang delicately traverse right. Going straight up over the overhang is 5.9; recommended.

3. EAST WALL ELIMINATE★ 5.9
Uses the diagonal crack and carefully avoids bigger holds to the right and left. The crux is a mantle onto a small ledge near the top.

4. NABISCO★★ 5.7
Either start from the previous route, better, or from a boulder further up, and head up the wall, on good holds, to a ledge. The crux is the slab above.

5. RH ROUTE★★ 5.8
The steep black wall on great holds and pin scars is followed by traversing up and right on the slippery slab; crux.

6. CHIMNEY★ 5.7
What better way to end the day? The chimney can also be gained from the left via a diagonal pin scarred crack.

7. MAGGIE'S TRAVERSE★★★ V1
From left to right. A long, long voyage from strenuous hanging to thin edging, to smearing on nothing. One of Stoney's best bouldering traverses. (And it's in the shade!)

8. IGUANA TRAVERSE★ V0
Start at Iguana but go left on large holds, the crux really needs a spot, finish at the end of the big holds, by the bush.

9. IGUANA★★ 5.11c
An undercling gains good holds (used to be better); head straight up on long reaches to a high step finish.

10. SCURF★★ 5.12
Well spaced positive holds, which get smaller every year, lead to rock which relents to merely vertical; side pulls lead to a pocket. The crux is reaching the horizontal break.

11. MAGGIE'S FARM★★★ 5.11b
Some people find this route harder than the other two. A puzzling start leads to hidden holds in the crack. Follow it to the right. From here a short wall leads to the pin scars; getting past these is the crux. Great stuff!

12. SPROUT WINGS & FLY★ 5.13?
The wall to the right of Maggie's.

Texas Flake

The large detached flake at the bottom of the west wall of the canyon (see Page 72).

TEXAS FLAKE FACE★ VB
The outside face of the detached flake; seams to easy slab.

TEXAS FLAKE OVERHANG★★ V2R
The overhanging inside face seems compelling. Can you muster on the friable holds?

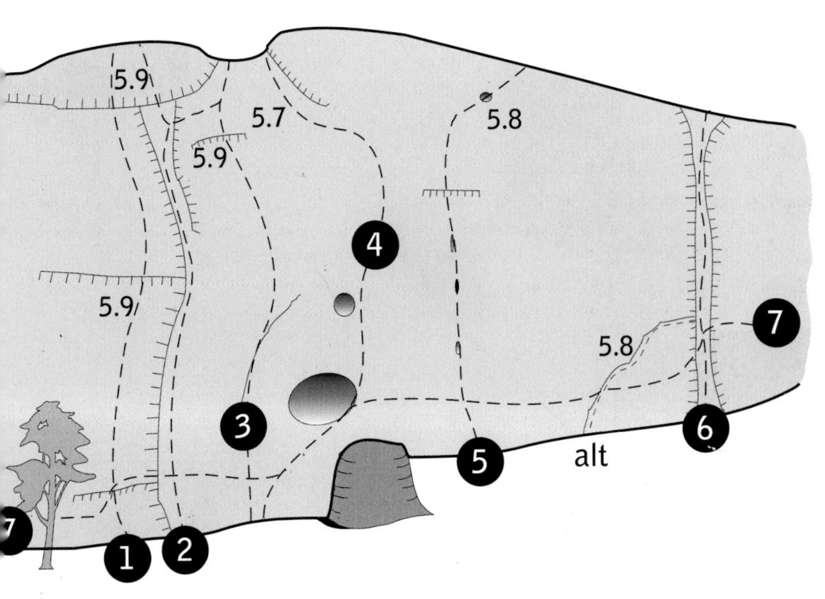

AST WALL

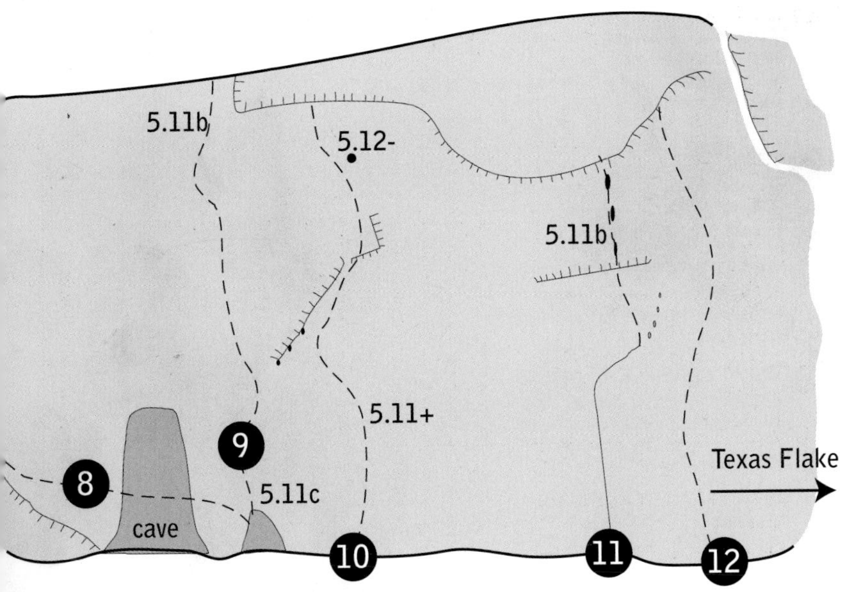

VEST WALL

Nutcracker Buttress

This narrow face is home to a Stoney classic. The same anchor facilitates several routes, all of them good. Use slings and nuts/cams. The easy way to the top involves heading up the canyon to the right over blocks. Route length 40′.

❶ **COSMIC CORNER** 5.10d
Traverse under the roof, and then up.

❷ **NUTCRACKER★★★** 5.10a
The scene of many failures, a classic. Head up on the left into an alcove, boldly step right, onto the bulge. The crux is moving up to the horizontal break. The crack above can be tricky too.

❸ **NUTCRACKER DIRECT★★** 5.11+
Start on the right and tackle the bulge direct on tiny holds, then join with the standard route.

❹ **747★★★** 5.10c
Starts around the corner. Head up to the left side of the bulge and make a cruncher move onto the hand-hold; after this the nose of the 747 is reached. Once over the nose a fingery slab makes a fitting finale.

A POCKETFUL OF TENDON-ITIS★ 5.10c
Slightly contrived, but good. Head up to the right, traverse right and, using pockets, climb up the steep wall to another Stoney bellyflop. Slightly loose.

NUTCRACKER CANYON TRAVERSE★ V1
Start at 747 and head up and right along the canyon wall. It gets very thin.

The Slab

To reach the top of the slab head up Nutcracker Canyon, then go right. Thread belay and one bolt, take a hanger. Route length 30′.

❺ **LEFT EDGE★** 5.9
Pull over the bulge then traverse left. Lieback moves lead to the top. Can be started on the left from the canyon.

❻ **HEART OF GLASS★** 5.9
The same start leads to a unique problem for Stoney; a slab with potato chip edges.

❼ **RIGHT EDGE★** 5.9
Step off a boulder on the right. This can also be used as an easy start for the other two routes. The crux is starting the edge.

Noreen Flynn at the crux of The O-Zone (Page 88)

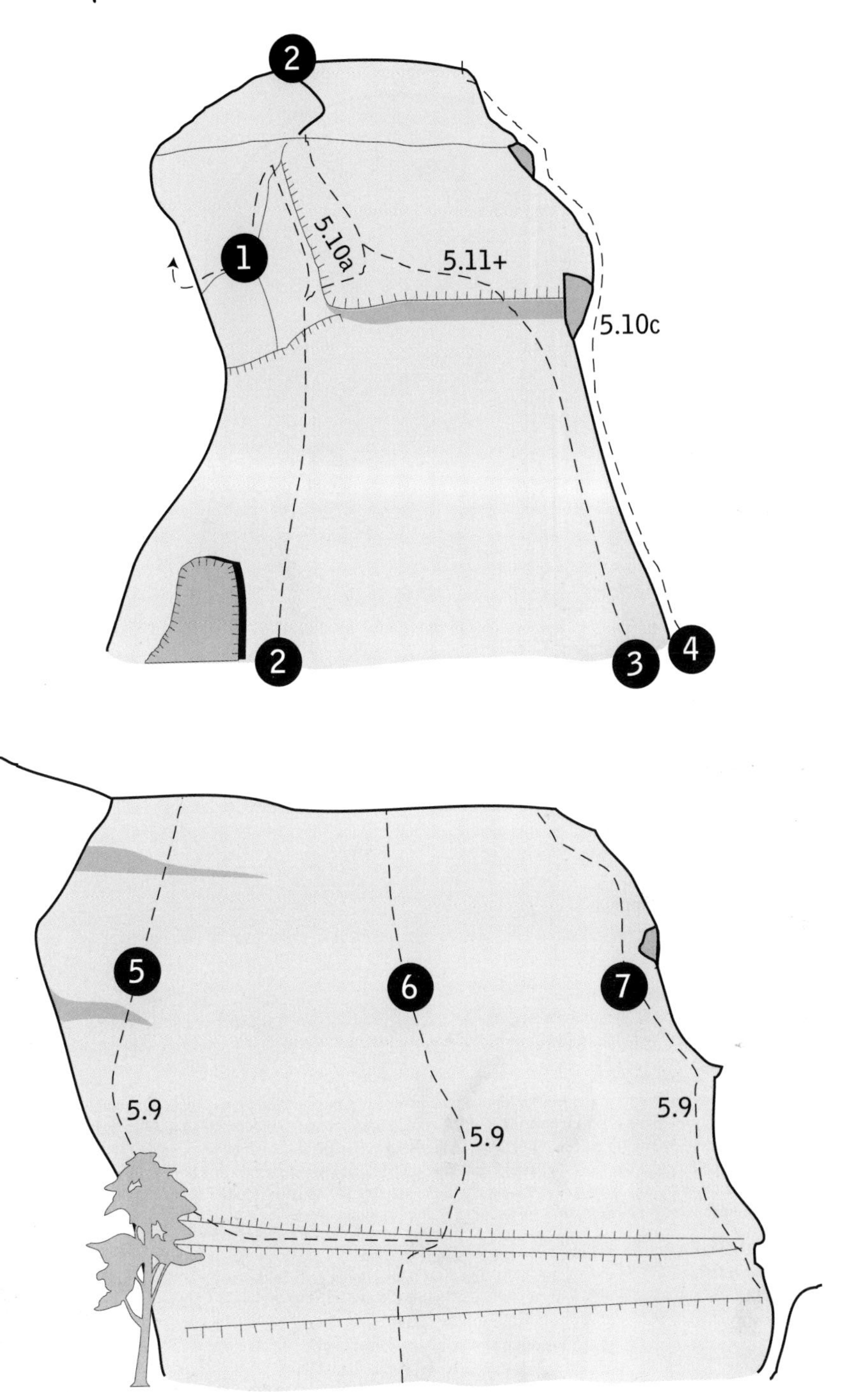
2
5.10a
5.11+
1
5.10c
2
3
4
5
6
7
5.9
5.9
5.9

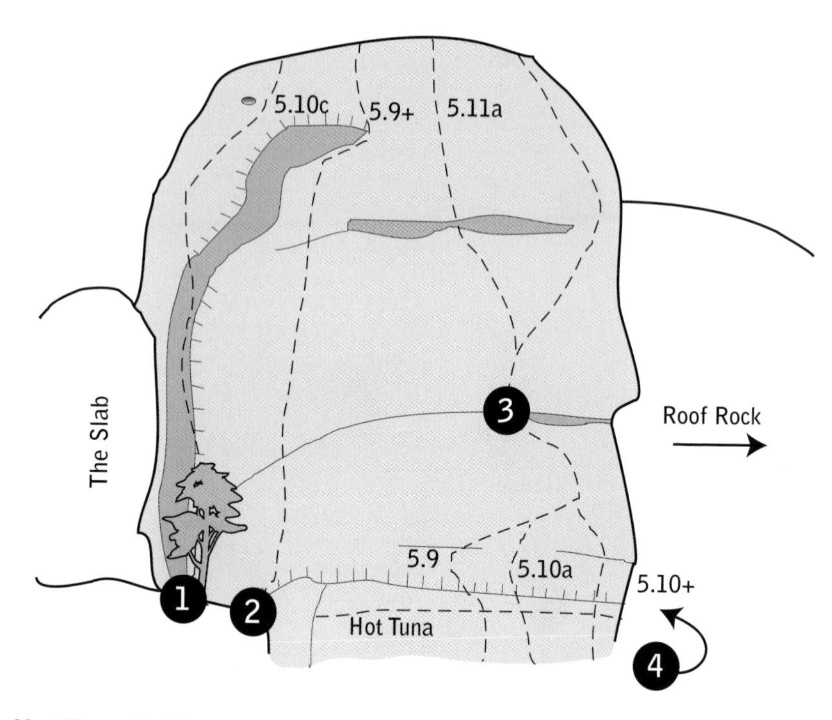

Hot Tuna Buttress

There's some good stuff here. The anchor requires some very long slings for the tree and a #10 hex behind the boulder on the right, take two hangers for the bolts. The chimney to the left of the face provides access to the top. Route length 40′.

❶ EAT OR BE EATEN★★★ 5.10c
Start up the corner, then step out left onto the face. Interesting moves lead up the edge to a "why did I come?" finish.

❷ THE O-ZONE★★ 5.9+
This good route has two variations, either up the corner to the overlap, or better, up the face to the right and directly up the bulge to the same place, a wild position. The crux is bypassing the overlap to the right.

❸ FLYING FISH★ 5.9
Start this climb with a jump from a boulder, the hold is big, once on the lip of Hot Tuna Roof either head up, or better, traverse right along the lip of the roof, a tough move over the second overlap leads to easy ground, finish up the rib on the right. **VARIATION I★** (5.10a) It's possible to get over the lip without the jump using holds to the right. **VARIATION II★** (5.10+) At the right hand end of the roof tall people can make another jump. Shorties need power and finesse (5.11a). **VARIATION FINISH★** (5.11a) Go up the wall to the left of the right-hand rib using small holds and pockets.

❹ COLD TURKEY★ 5.11b/c
Around to the right, in the alcove. A hard mantle over a bulge (can be a boulder problem too) leads to sandy climbing up to another bulge, strenuous moves lead past this; loose holds, to easier climbing.

oof Rock

's is the last big buttress on the north side, it sees very little top-rope traffic; the top-rope anchor is tricky to , long slings are needed, a small cam placed in a pocket near the edge helps to stop the rope from sliding over. e canyon to the right is the way to the top. Route length 40′.

LEFT CRACK★ 5.8
This crack can be led. Pass the roof using the crack and follow it all the way, past a tricky move left; be sure to finish up the flake on the right.

SANDSTORM★ 5.9
Use the same start as the previous climb but lieback up the crack in the wall to reach pockets.

FLAKESTORM★★ 5.9+
The same crack as before; then traverse right to the edge of the wall, which is overhanging, up this quickly to a ledge, finish up the slab above. It's a pity it's so short. Now bolted, but should be chopped.

STORMWARNING★ 5.10c
Starts on top of the big detached boulder, a horizontal move, or screaming dyno, leads to good holds on the arete.

LAND SHARK 5.11b/c
Climbs up pockets on the wall around the corner.

THE SHARK'S TOOTH 5.10b/c
Lies to the right of the previous route.

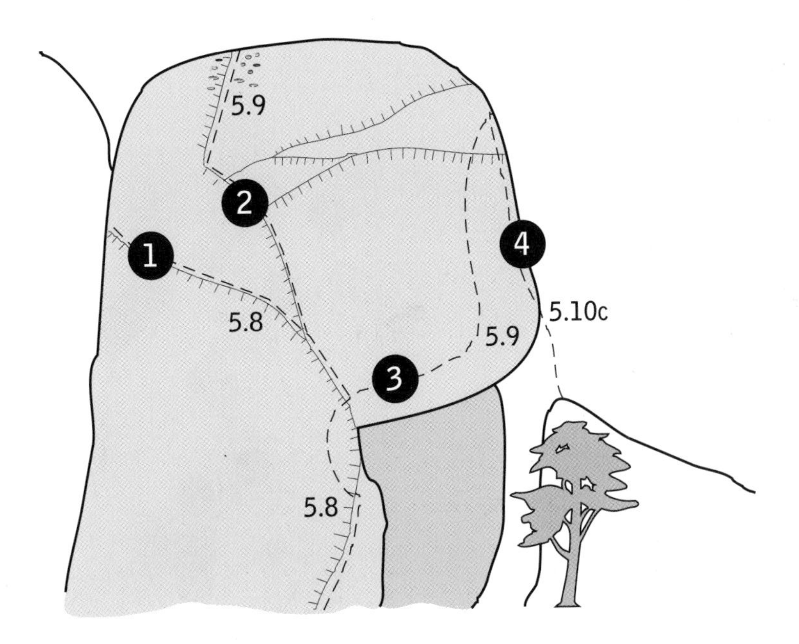

Hot Tuna Area Boulder Problems

The problems around Hot Tuna Buttress and Roof Rock are included here.

1 HOT TUNA★★★ V5
This Stoney classic lies beneath the roof, it's basically a very long and strenuous roof, see Pages 2-3.

2 SEAM V2R
Big flat hold to right facing seam, finish in cave, traverse off left.

3 MANTLE PROBLEM V5
Up and over the overhang using a ledge with not so good holds.

4 MICKEY MOUSE★★★ V5R
Start in Route 1 of Roof Rock but swing out left onto the bulge, then up this on slopers.

5 UNDERCLING TRAVERSE V1
Undercling the crack of Roof Rock either way, across and then down. The roof crack also goes at V5.

6 ROOF & ARETE V0
Big boulder. The low roof (Sit Start) then the grainy arete.

7 CRACK HAND-TRAVERSE★ V0R
The horizontal finger crack to step down onto boulder.

8 REARDON'S POCKET★ V5
Just right of the chimney, use the left pocket, and edge.

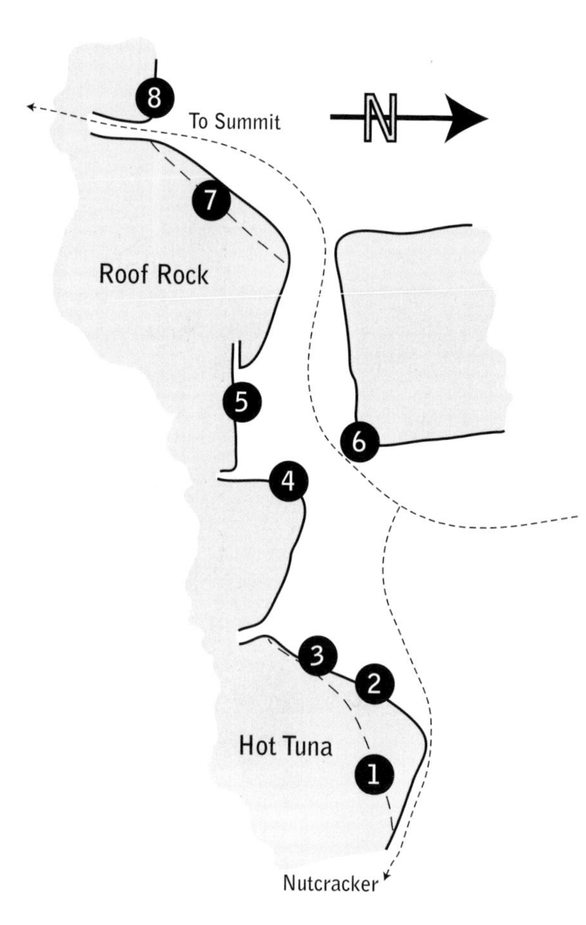

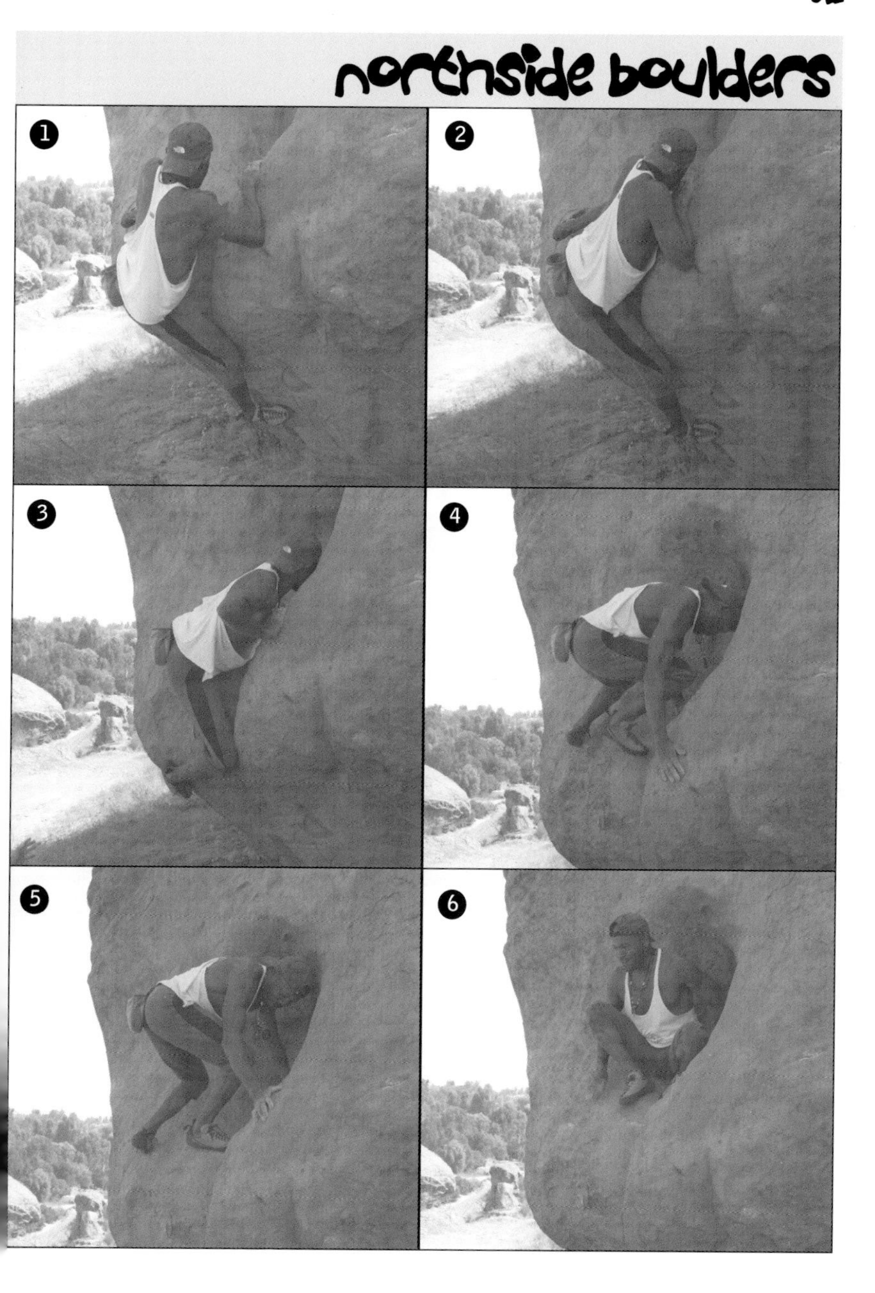

Tony Tennessee and MAJOR beta on Chouinard's Hole V2(Page 100)

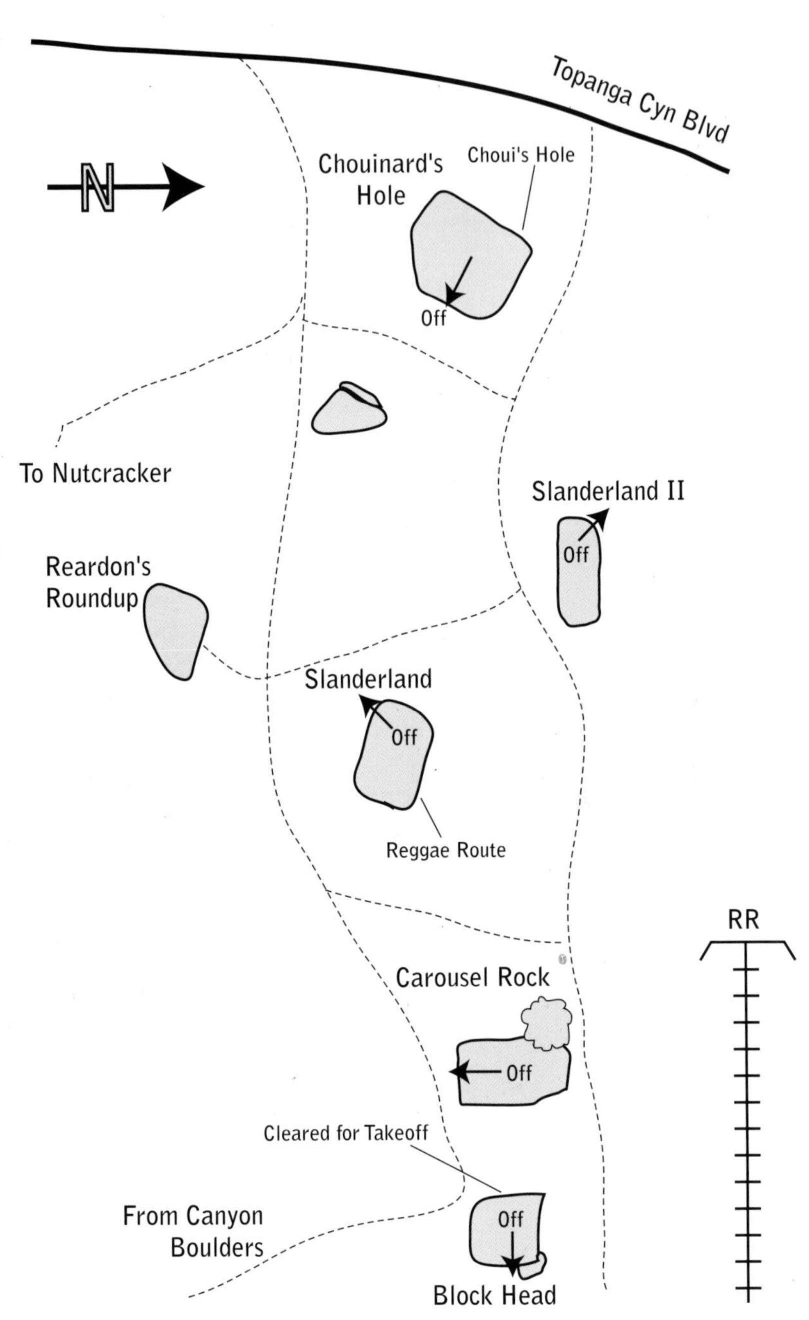

NORTHSIDE BOULDERS AREA

Block Head

AKA Snocone, Mushroom Boulder or Router Rock. A trio of hallmark hard routes give this boulder all the character it needs no matter what you call it.

CLEARED FOR TAKEOFF★ V3R
(See Page 92). A little loose and a lot reachy. A Ryan Murphy reinvention.

❶ YABO ARETE★★★ V8
Left hand on reachy pocket, high step and lunge up and right. Slopers and a pocket up high lead to a pure mantle on the top. Highball over rocky landing. Height dependent start.

❷ THE ROUTER BIT★ V5
Start on lowest chipped holds (years ago, a production company defaced the rock with a router bit, hence the name), then up to sloper in middle of face and head left. Top out directly.

❸ LARGONAUT★★ V6
Standing start on block with right hand on edge is the original route by John Long. Sit start with left hand on low edge by Jeff Johnson, and height dependent (V7). Follow the slopers and micro edges directly up.

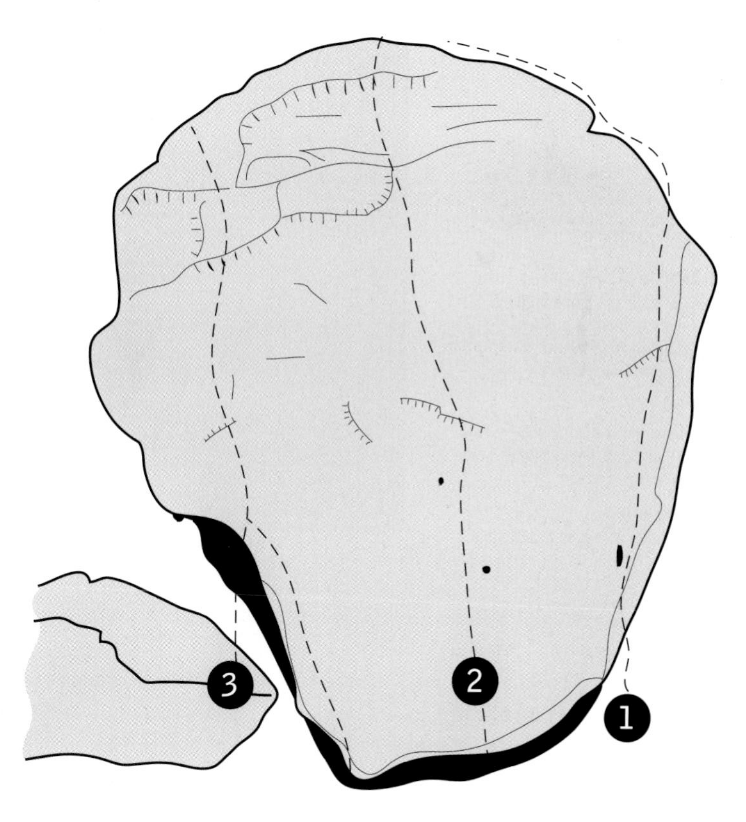

NORTH SIDE

Carousel Rock

The rock on the west side is not as solid as one would wish for, and holds break off, so (ignoring the unforgivable chipped holds) these routes tend to get trickier. The easiest way up (or down) is a Class 5 on the south side, the holds are a little loose, there are bolts if you're top-roping. Route length 30′.

1 THE ROLLERCOASTER★★ V2R (5.11 TR)
Gain the pocket and traverse to the left, getting on the small ledge is the crux and can prove quite baffling, finish up the very thin face. **VARIATION START★★** (V1) Start left of the previous route and head up the rib to a ledge, one more move reaches the previous route at the baffling crux. **VARIATION START II** (V1) Start left of the rib, climb straight up to a pocket then step right and onto the baffling crux ledge.

2 SANCTUARY V0 (5.10b TR)
Same start as Var.II but go left and finish up the tricky wall. Warning! Bees.

3 CAROUSEL FACE★ VB
The left side of the face using large holds.

4 CAROUSEL EDGE★ VB
Dyno up the overhanging arete.

CAVE★ V2R
Directly out of the cave and up the center. Scary top out.

5 SW CORNER★★★ V0
Sequence to a diagonal flake, then pull right and finish.

6 FACE★ V2
Sidepulls to an undercling, reach for crimp, creepy top out.

7 MANTLE PROBLEM★ V5
Slap for diagonal handrail, jog up and then using a small pocket slap for the top and mantle.

8 CRACK V0
Climb up past the diagonal handrail and finish up the crack. **VARIATION** (V0) start as for the next route, undercling over and up the crack.

9 SLAB★ V0
Crux face moves off the ground lead to the undercling, step left and follow the flake.

10 FACE★ V0
Crimps behind the tree to left sloper, mantle up.

Stefan Harms finishes up SW Corner V0

11 ARETE★ V1
The right of the arete on tiny holds and using the edge. **LEFT OF ARETE** (V2) also goes.

12 NORTH FACE★ V5
Use the skull shaped pocket to gain access to an okay crimp. Jog up to slap a nice jug on the lip.

13 TRAVERSE OF CAROUSEL ROCK★★★ V5
Thin slabs, thin edges, dynos; the works. As the holds vanish it gets harder and harder.

14 NIGHT TRAIN★★★ V5
Up to the undercling then the face direct above it - M.Reardon & T.Bristow.

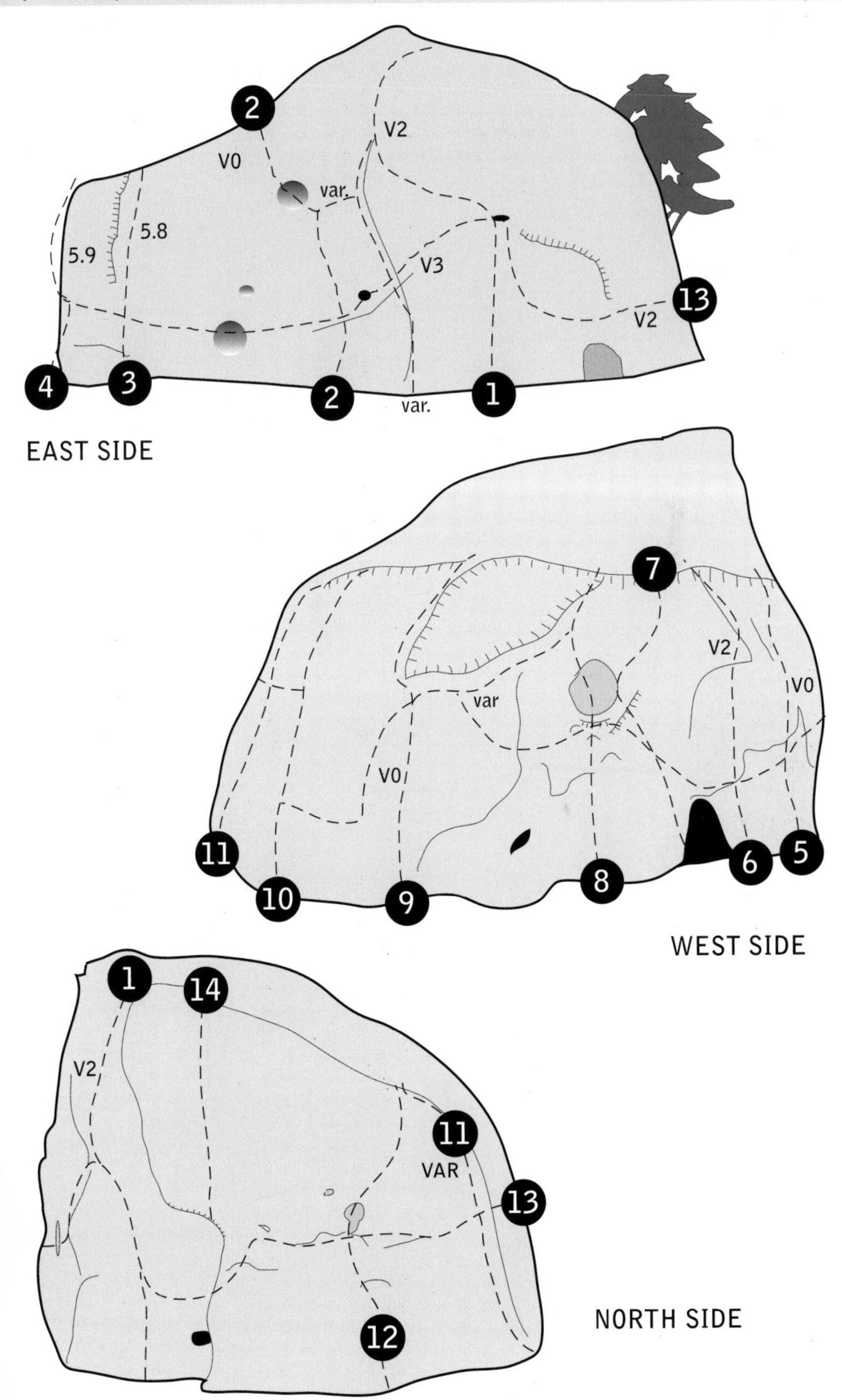
2
V2
V0
var.
5.8
5.9
V3
13
V2
4
3
2
var.
1
EAST SIDE
7
V2
V0
var
V0
11
10
9
8
6
5
WEST SIDE
1
14
V2
11
VAR
13
12
NORTH SIDE

Slanderland

Getting to the top is a real adventure! If you don't mind bouldering, you can solo to the top up Reggae Route; or throw a rope over the top then go up the slab. There are bolts on top. Route length 35′.

1. **SLANDERLAND** V1
The steep face on less than solid holds.

2. **BAD PRESS** V5
Middle of the face, sit start.

3. **TROUBLE TOLD★★** V0
A big pull followed by a lieback of the flake.

4. **THE 5.9 SLAB★** 5.10c
Top rope or lead with 2 bolts. Traverse right to the edge; tricky, even trickier moves lead up past the bolts to easier ground. A fall before clipping the 2nd bolt may deposit you on the ground.

5. **THE 5.10 SLAB** 5.11a
Another hard slab on very indefinite, grainy holds.

6. **HOLY S^^T★** 5.10d
Up and left to a steep section, technical and delicate moves lead to easier stuff.

7. **REGGAE ROUTE★★** V1 (5.10+)
A problematical start on chopped holds leads to the crux, a delicate move; after that it's easier.

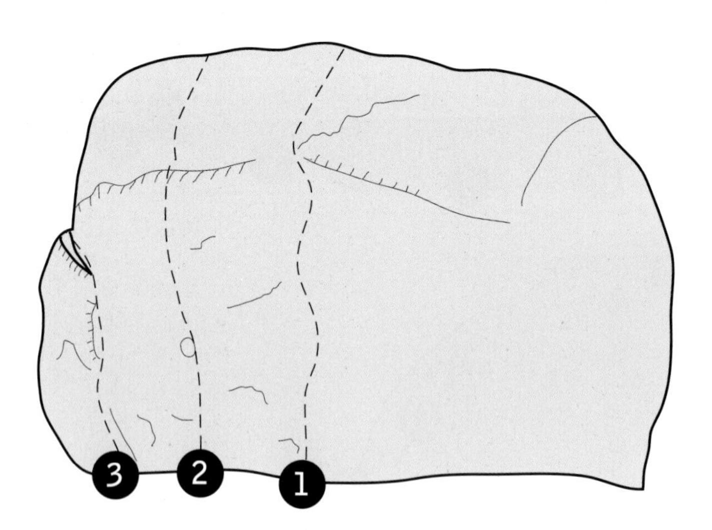

SLANDERLAND SOUTH SIDE

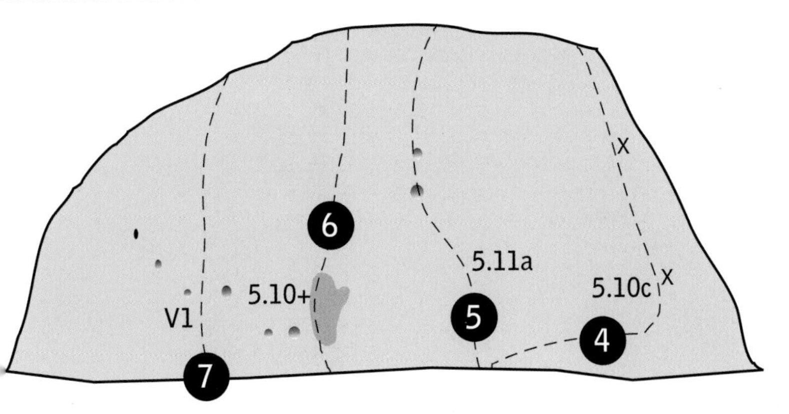

SLANDERLAND NORTH SIDE

Reardon's Roundup

There's a low boulder south of Slanderland, across the trail, home to some short, hard, testpieces.

1. UNNAMED★ V8
The left problem.

2. WOOL: TOM'S OTHER USE FOR SHEEP★ V7
The middle problem.

3. BRISTOW'S BITCH★★ V5
The right problem is deceptively difficult.

4. HEFFER LOVIN' COWBOY★★ V4
Start at Route (3) and head right around the corner to a pocket, then up.

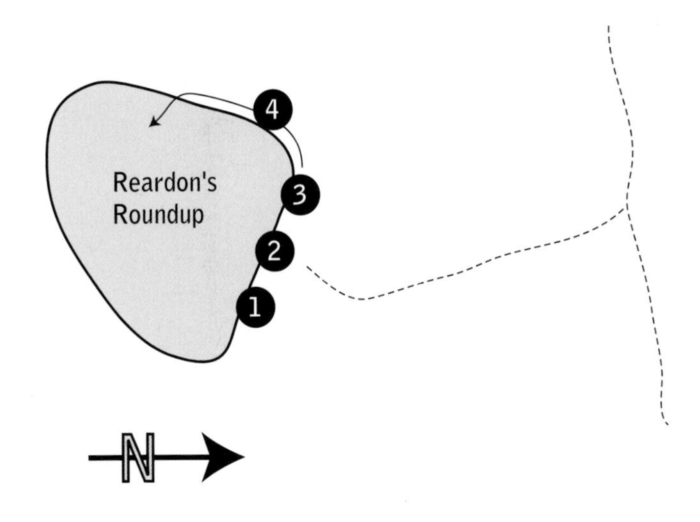

Fred Batliner on Alice in Slanderland V1

Slanderland II

Located just north of the previous boulder, the easiest way to the top is to solo the chopped holds up the slab on the north side. Bolt anchors on top; take hangers. Route length 30′

1 ROUTE RUSTLIN′★ 5.10+
The steep climb on the left.

2 YARD THE TOOL★ 5.10a/b
Steep with a tricky finish.

3 ALICE IN SLANDERLAND★★ V1
From the tree around to the NE corner. At the chopped holds (argh!) on the north side go down. Very crimpy crux.

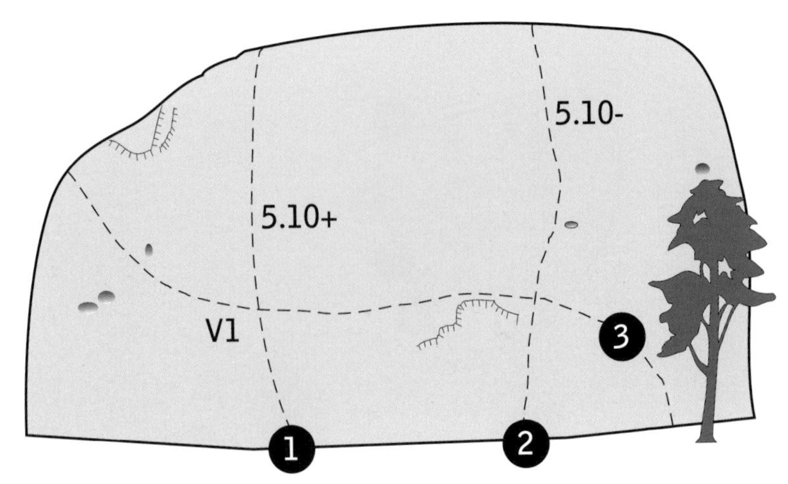

SOUTH SIDE

Boulder South of Chouinard's Hole

Quite a few short but fun routes here. Descend down the slab on the north side.

1. CRACK VB
Up the flake to a ledge, then onto the top.

2. SLAB★ V0
Thin smearing for a couple of moves to the ledge on the previous route.

3. BULGE V0
Sidepull and crimpers, then delicately onto the slab.

4. OVERHANGING FACE V5
Trend left from jugs onto crimps and not so good holds, then shoot for lip.

5. DON'T GIVE ME NO LIP★ V0
From the creaky jugs, a controlled throw to lip then over.

6. VENGABOYS★ VB
Pocket and flake, to step over lip.

7. WE LIKE TO PARTY★ VB
A one move problem off a couple of good holds and thin feet.

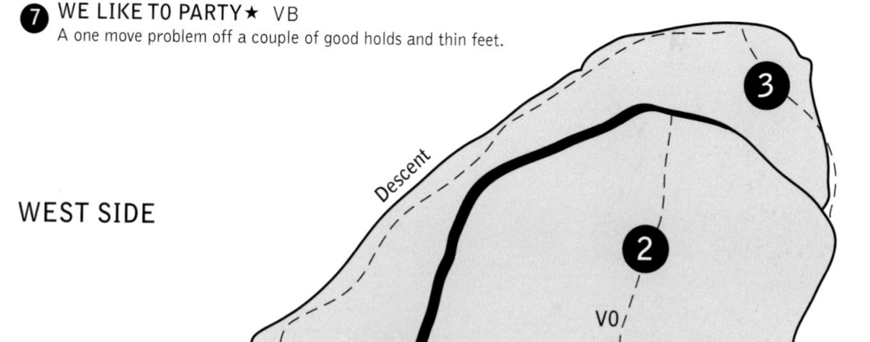

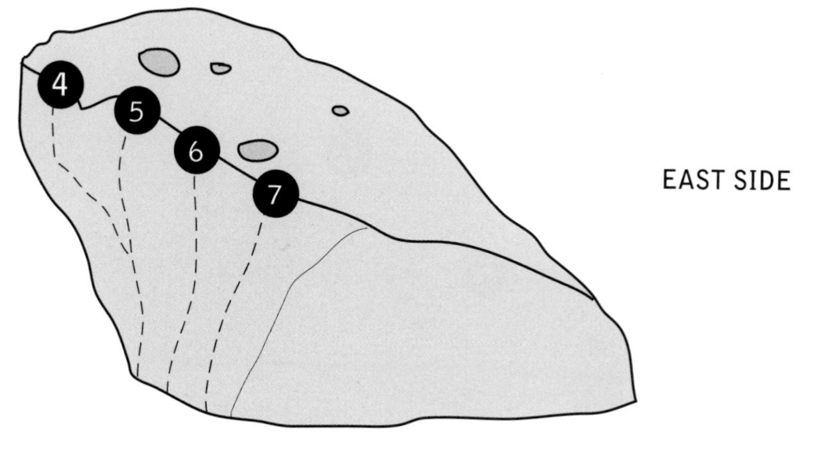

Chouinard's Hole

Very large boulder close to Topanga Canyon Boulevard. Descend down Route 5 then jump.

1. **ARETE ME NOT★★** V5
   A great line. Lieback up the overhanging arete just left of Chouinard's Hole. There's a sit start too (V?).
2. **CHOUINARD'S HOLE★★★** V2
   Sandbag. Get up into the hole, turn around and sit down (photo on Page 91).
3. **HALF GRAM★** V7
   Very powerful overhanging mantle, jump off or continue up slab.
4. **BUSH DOCTOR** V2
   Flakes to large pothole then slab?
5. **BONEHOLE★** V0
   Tricky thin start to easier but high slab.
6. **STANDARD ROUTE** VB
   Up pockets to the slab.

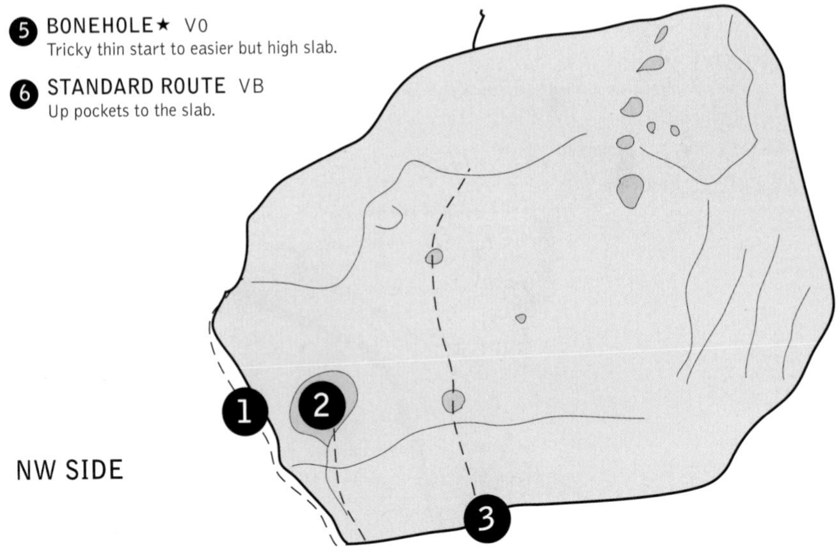

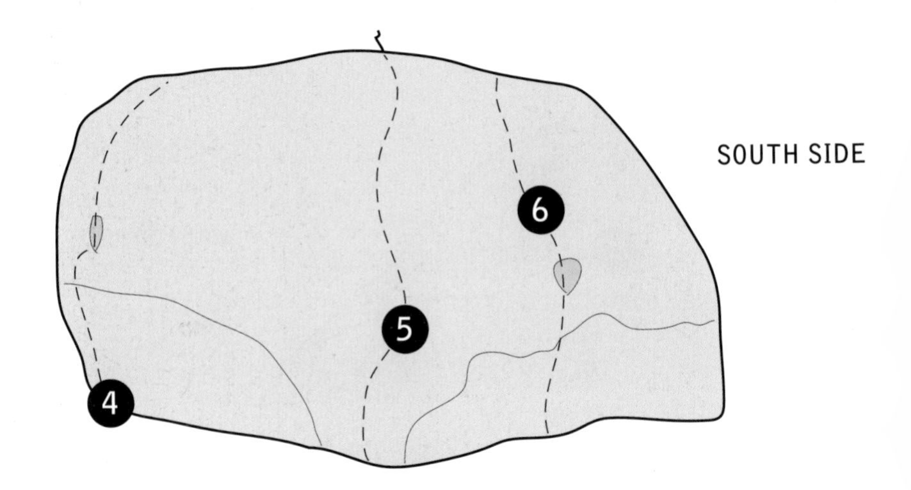

west walls

Noreen Flynn eases towards the diagonal pockets on Jesus Wall 5.10c (Page 107)

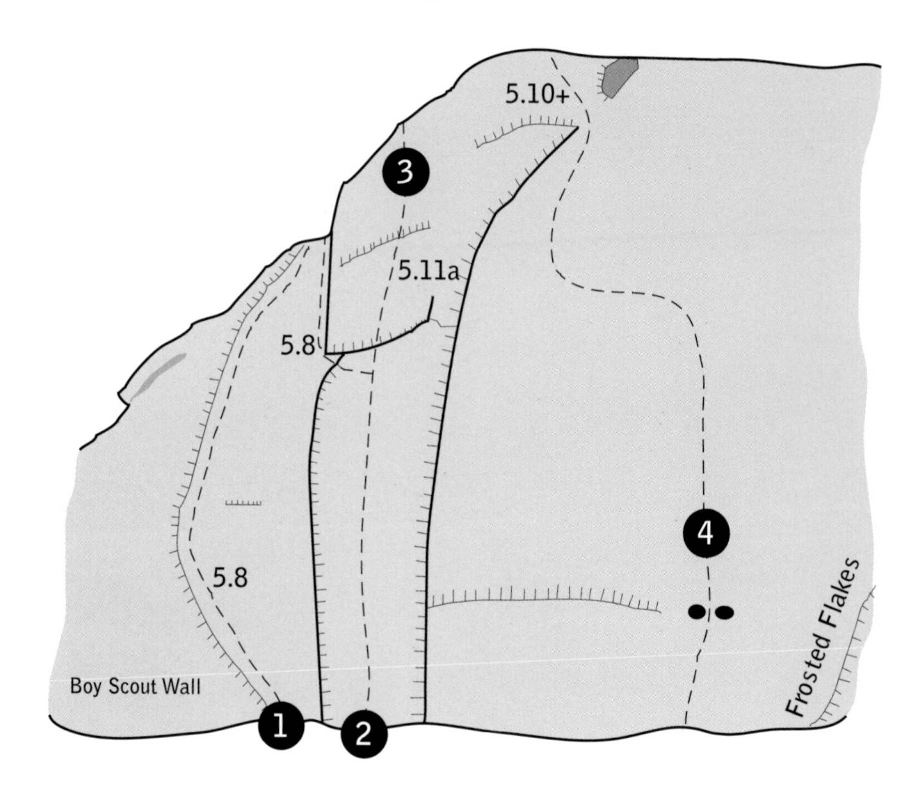

Suburbia

This is located close to the north west corner, the top can be gained by going around the corner to the left, cross a slab and head up a gully and step over a crevasse. Very long slings are required for the anchors. Route length 45′.

1 LEFTHAND CRACK★ 5.8
Follow the ramp left and finish up the crack, or better, traverse right along an undercling to finish.

2 PEDESTAL CRACK★ 5.8
Climb to the top of The Pedestal a tricky step left leads to the exposed crack.

3 KAIRO★ 5.11a
From the top of The Pedestal the wall above can be overcome using an off balance mantle.

4 NORTHWEST PASSAGE★ 5.10+
A good steep face leads to the overhang, the crux is getting over this section, which is a real puzzler!

AREA MAP ON PAGE 108

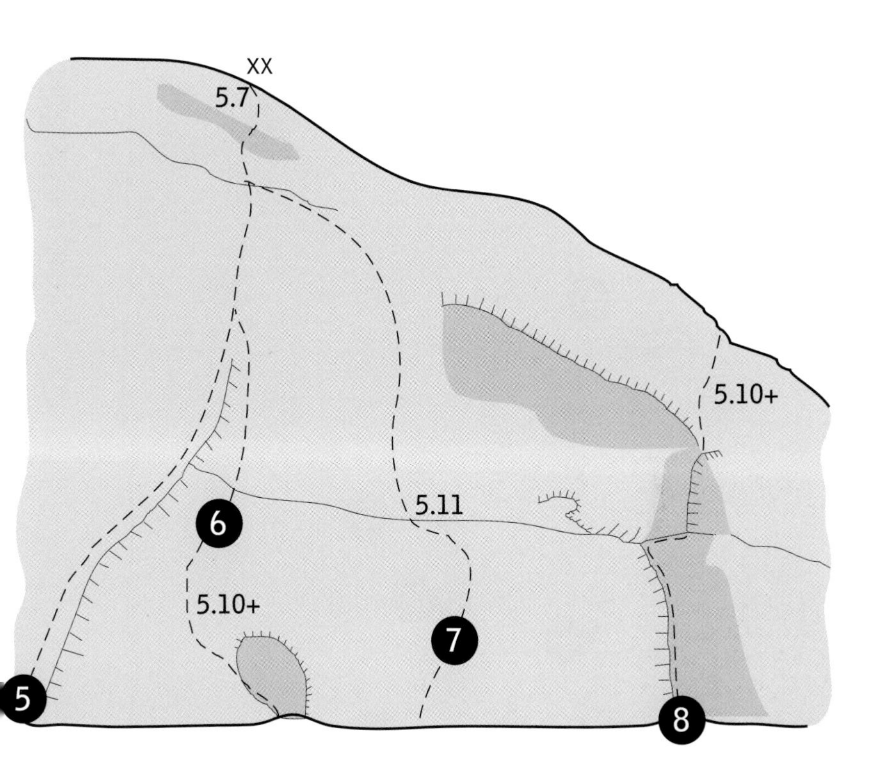

5 **FROSTED FLAKES★★★** 5.7
A classic moderate route up the black section of rock, the finish is the crux; a fiendish mantle.

6 **TONY THE TIGER★★** 5.10+
Starts just right of the previous route. Climb up bulging rock, eventually jôining Frosted Flakes.

7 **CIRCUS GAMES★** 5.11
Climb the steep wall using pockets and flakes, getting past the overhang is the crux.

8 **SWEET SUBURBIA★★** 5.10+
An intimidating route. Climb up the rotten corner then make a committing traverse right, lieback up the overhanging crack and climb the wall above (crux) on dubious holds.

Other Suburbia Routes

Boy Scout Wall to the left of Suburbia Wall has some interesting short top rope problems, 5.7/5.8. There are also some top rope routes located in the crevasse encountered during the approach to the top. Both walls have been climbed; the routes range from 5.7 on the left to 5.11 on the right-hand wall. However, this place smells of guano and has a lot of trash.

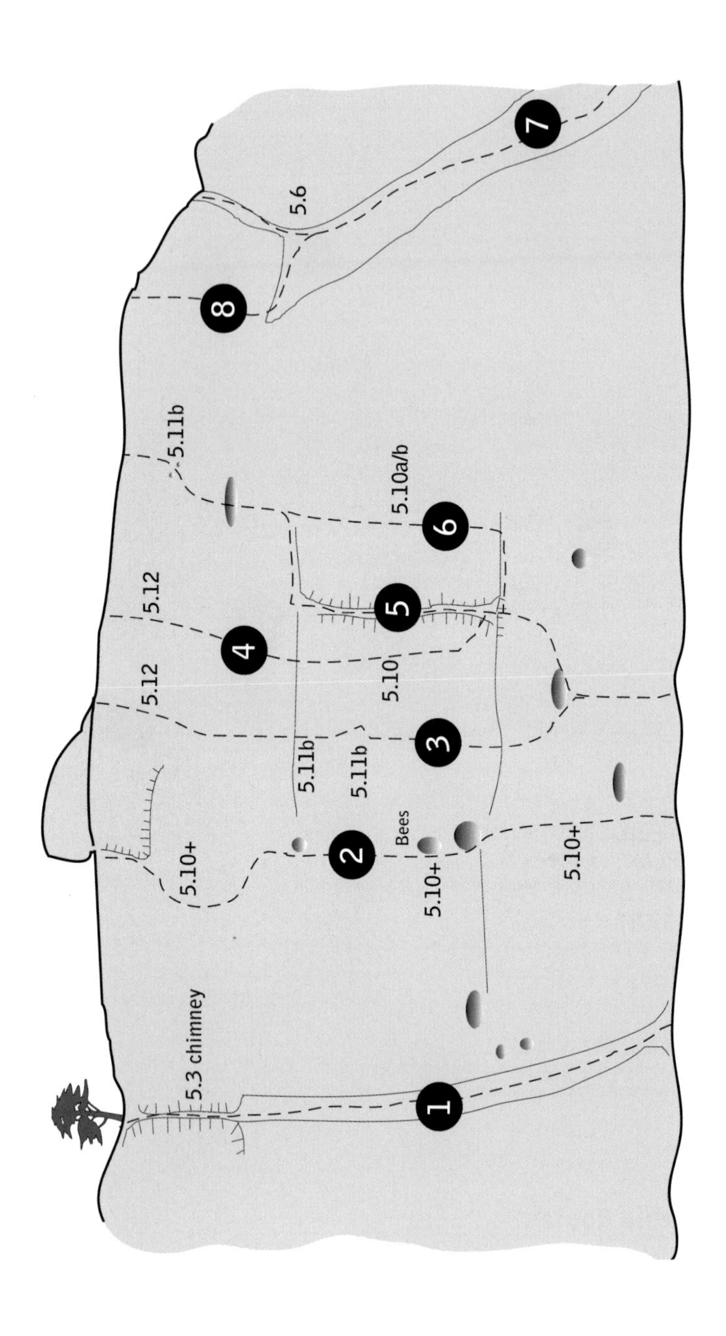

AREA MAP ON PAGE 108

The Main Wall

This is the highest piece of rock at Stoney Point. Not much action seen here so watch out for loose holds. The steep face makes for some pretty intense climbing. To reach the top; either solo up the S-Crack or go up the broken buttress to the right (the same approach as The Jesus Wall and The Pillar). Long slings and nuts/cams make up the anchors. Use a 60 or 70m rope. Route length 80′.

❶ S-CRACK★★★ 5.4
An excellent beginners route on the left margin of the wall. The crux is the chimney at the top. Usually led.

❷ KILLER BEES★ 5.10+
Do this one on a cold morning, when the bees aren't so angry! Start to the right of S-Crack at a small round pocket. Climb up into a scoop and make a weird mantle, the first crux, the rock is loose but stick with it because it improves higher up, gain the ledge by the bees nest and climb the slightly overhanging wall to the left of it (or lieback up the honeycomb); the second crux. The next section is easier and a Thank God ledge provides a welcome rest, traverse left along this and step onto a foothold which leads to an undercling, the third crux involves gaining the blank slab, easier climbing leads past the corner to the top.

❸ MAIN WALL★★ 5.12
The next four routes tackle the wall and share the same start. Using pockets and flakes gain the scoop; good, hard, face climbing leads up this over a slight bulge to a ledge. The pocketed face above starts out well then turns the cold shoulder with a boulder problem finish, suspended above the abyss (crux).

❹ I HAVE FAITH★★ 5.12
Start in the same place as the previous climb but head right aiming for a ledge at the bottom of the obvious vee groove. Step out left onto the wall and in a great position head straight up, then trend right for the crux finish on sloping pockets.

❺ PICK POCKET★ 5.11b
From the groove ledge; up the groove then traverse right to a good ledge beneath another pocketed face, leaving the last two pockets is the crux.

❻ OZYMANDIAS★★★ 5.11b
An awesome wall climb. Move right from the vee groove ledge and steep exposed climbing (5.10b) leads up the black face. The crux is the same finish as Pick Pocket.

❼ THE MAIN CHIMNEY★ 5.6
Up the dihedral and over the bulge, much easier climbing leads to the crux; up and right over a little wall to gain the slab above. This is a lead.

❽ VARIATION FINISH 5.11
(TR) Instead of going right at the little wall, go to the left of the overhang and finish up using pockets.

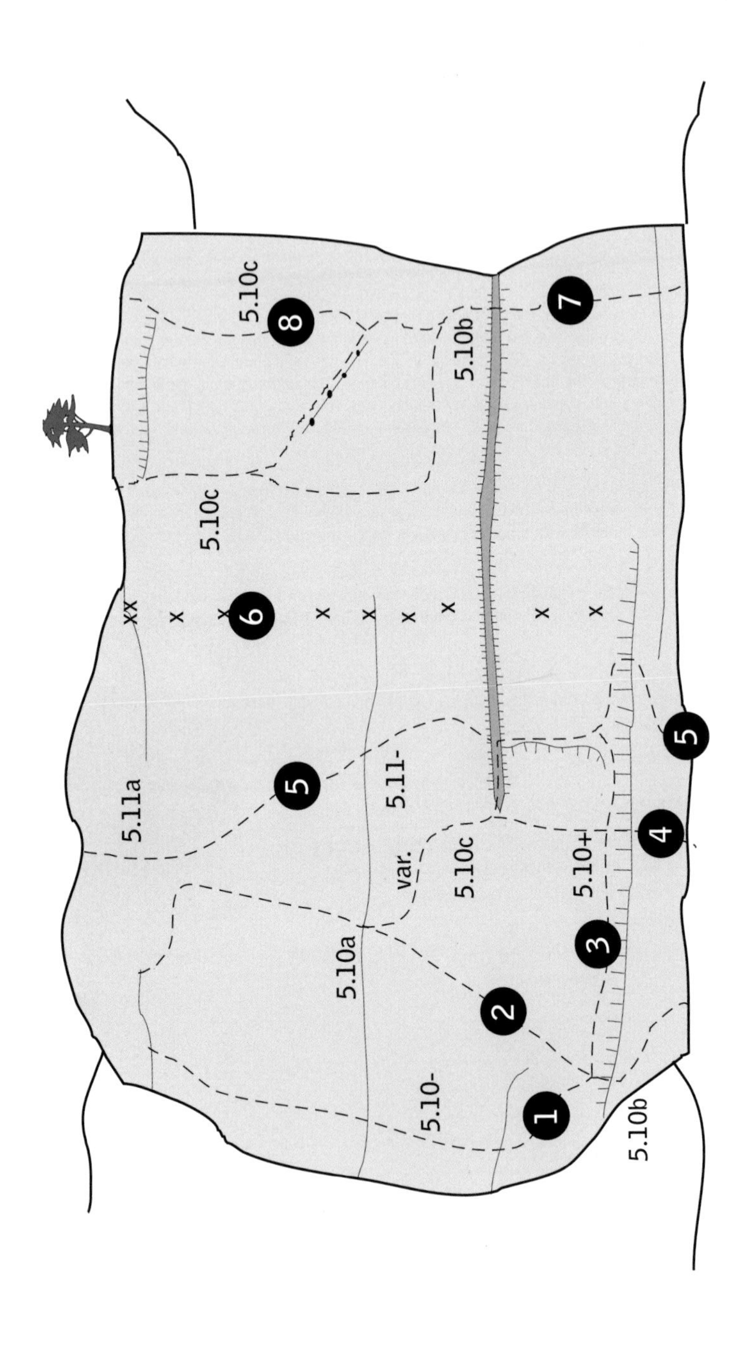

AREA MAP ON PAGE 108

The Jesus Wall

This wall is not quite as steep as The Main Wall. The holds are smaller however and the routes are long, delicate, exposed and highly recommended. Approach the top from the right, up the broken buttress and the tricky little wall, then go to the left; a tree, slings, nuts and cams make up the anchor. Route length 70′.

1 LEFT EDGE★★ 5.10b
Strenuous moves over the overhang lead to face climbing up the left edge of the wall. Finish by traversing left into the top of Main Chimney.

2 JESUS WALL LEFT★★★ 5.10c
The same start as the previous climb but trend right and up the depression in the wall, great moves lead up this to the final headwall; traverse left to finish up the arete or finish up Route (5).

3 VARIATION I★ 5.9
Traverse right to connect with Central Route.

4 VARIATION II★ 5.10+
Climb up over the little roof - loose - and pick a route.

5 CENTRAL ROUTE★★★ 5.11a
A delicate and intense climb just to the left of the old bolt ladder. Mantle onto a ledge then go left to a crack, this leads to a ledge (possible to toe traverse left to join Jesus Wall Left from here, another good variation) from here go up and right then straight up to the crux headwall, bouldering moves lead to a sandy crack and then the top. Fantastic!!

6 BOLT LADDER 5.6, C1
Stoney's last remaining aid route is this manky bolt ladder use it at your peril. Easy free climbing leads to the first hangerless bolt. Pro: Gear for 17 bolts, several rivet hangers.

7 JESUS WALL★★★ 5.10c
This climb has changed over the years; it used to go up just right of the bolt ladder. Missing holds have made this more difficult and the climb is usually started on the right side of the wall; from a ledge above the overlap either traverse left to reach better holds or head up to reach a diagonal line of pockets (sweet), follow these left and finish up the wall above on dubious holds.

8 CRUCIFIX★★ 5.10b/c
A variation finish. Instead of going left using the pockets; go straight up on loose holds; a little steeper.

THE CRACK 5.8
A nasty hand crack on the right.

LITTLE JESUS★ 5.9/5.10a
Climbs the wall to the right of the crack.

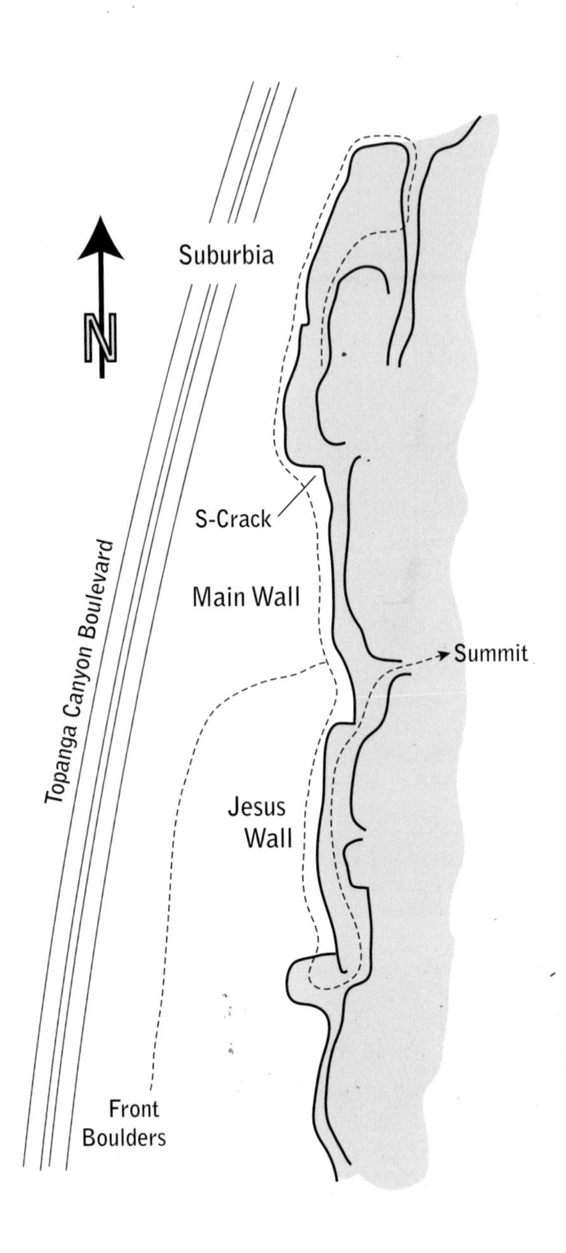

WEST WALLS (Routes on Pages 102 - 107).

A feline Melody Wong follows the Track of the Cat V0 (Page 113)

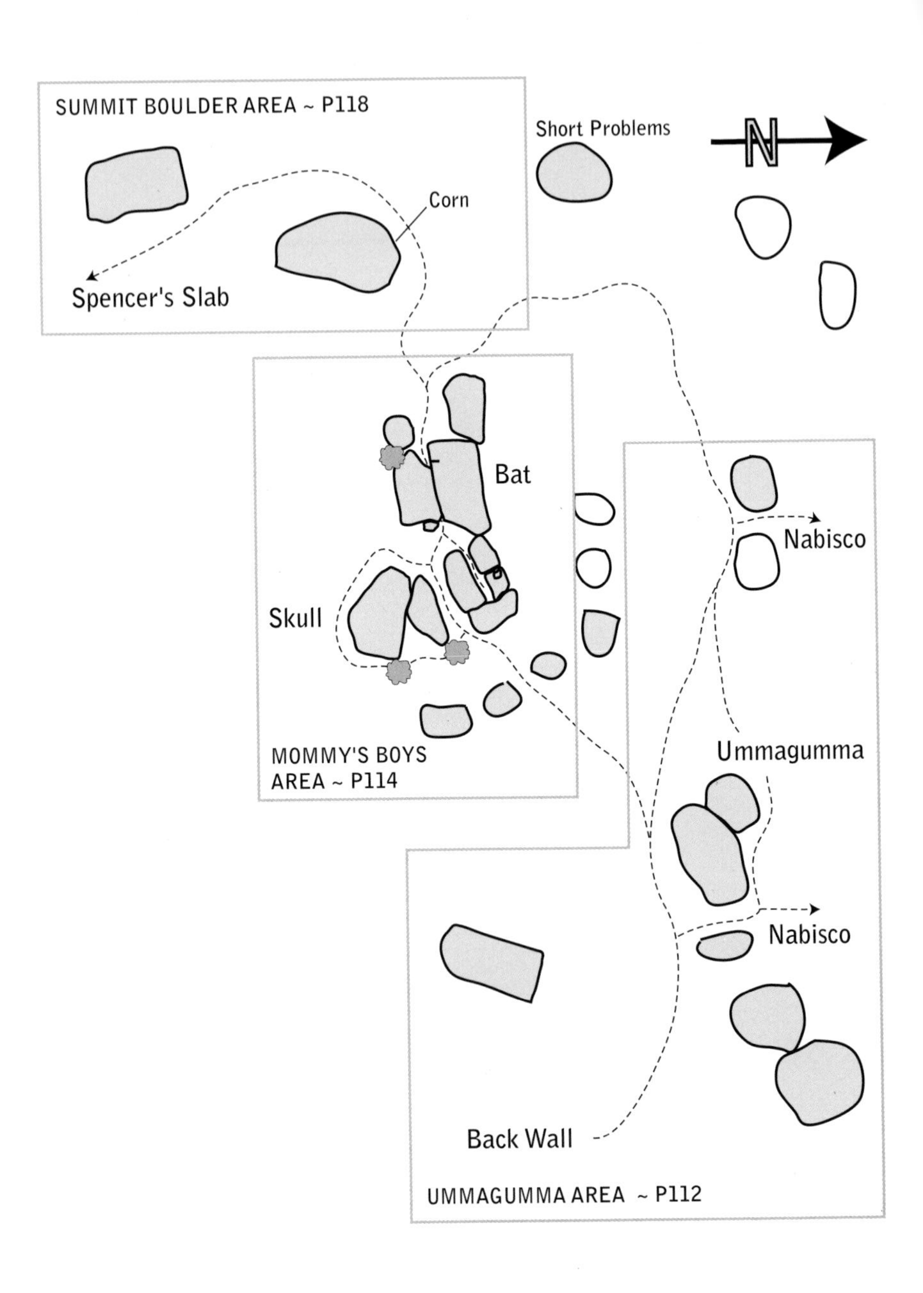

SUMMIT BOULDERS

Ummagumma

Home to Bachar's sought-after testpiece. See map on Page 112.

❶ **FACE★** V0
Thin face to the left of Ummagumma Crack.

❷ **UMMAGUMMA CRACK★** V0
A stiff little move leads to jamming then good holds. Has its moments.

❸ **HEIN FLAKE** V3
The start of Ummagumma Crack followed by a step right and up the indistinct flake.

❹ **TRAVERSE★** V4
From the crack to Hein Flake and across to Guarglophone.

❺ **GUARGLOPHONE★★** V4
Thin face to the left of Ummagumma.

❻ **UMMAGUMMA★★★** V7
Dynamic moves from one pocket to another followed by a right exit. As a variation go left to finger pocket and finish.

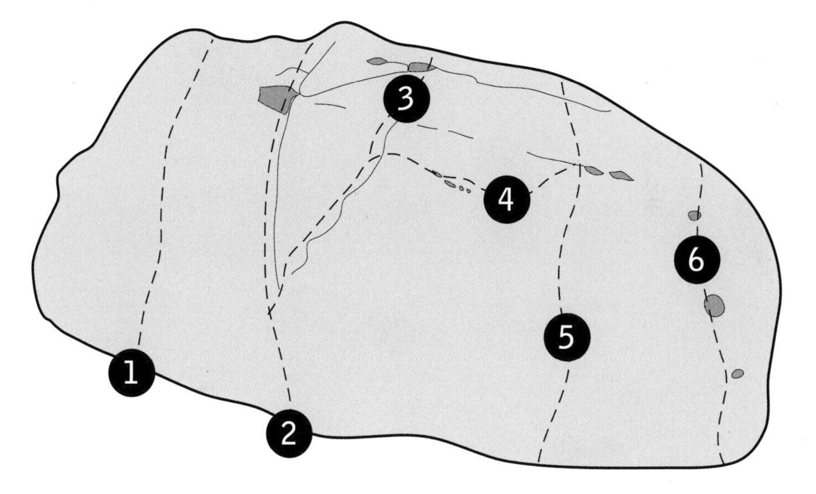

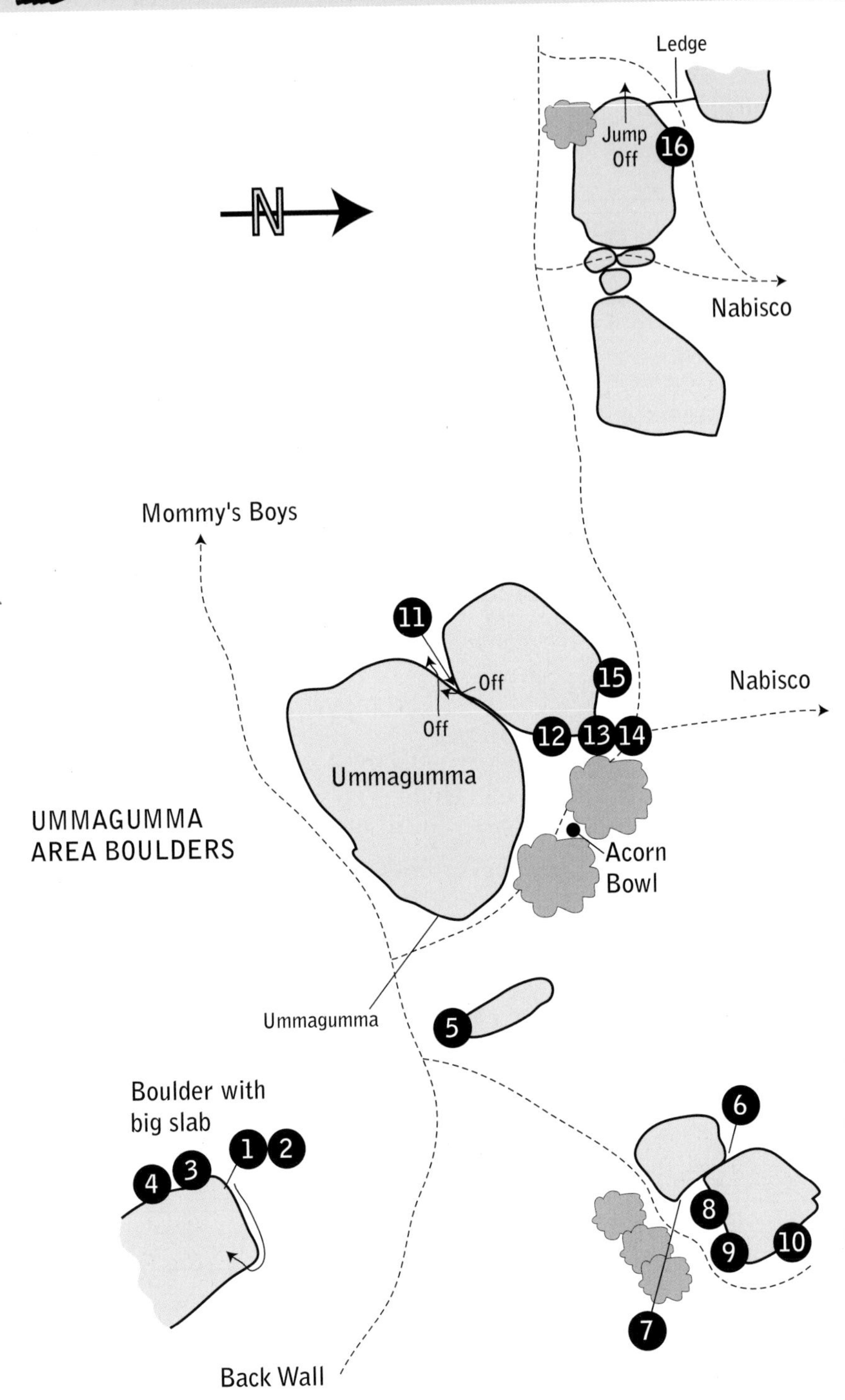
Ledge
Jump Off
16
N
Nabisco
Mommy's Boys
11
Off
Off
15
Nabisco
12
13
14
Ummagumma
UMMAGUMMA
AREA BOULDERS
Acorn Bowl
Ummagumma
5
Boulder with big slab
1
2
3
4
6
8
9
10
7
Back Wall

Jmmagumma Area Problems

he problems listed below are to be found on boulders near Ummagumma. There still seems to be some potential ere for people willing to explore. The Cave has been a well known secret amongst locals for a very long time. ɩs you pass to the right of the Ummagumma problem (Page 111) and under the trees heading towards the cave ɿere's an acorn grinding bowl carved into the bedrock next to a California Live Oak; a little piece of American rehistory, respect it. *Yair Kuperstein added some excellent hard test-pieces here.

1 MANTLES V0
Two pockets on the lip allow a mantle, more mantles to the left, harder.

2 LIP TRAVERSE★ V2
Start at (1) but do a lip traverse around the corner and up the arete.

3 FACE & SLAB I★ VB
Rounded flake followed by slab.

4 FACE & SLAB II★ V0
Thinner face to the right of the rounded flake followed by slab.

5 THE HAWK V4
Opposite Ummagumma. Smears on the arete lead to a mantle finish.

6 STICKY FINGERS★ V1
From north to south. Where the two boulders meet. Hand and fist jam out of the arch, jam and stem up to finish.

7 INCUBATOR★ V6
*Just left of the cave, sit and big undercling to slopers, then jam over the cave - strenuous.

8 FACE★ V3
Steep face on side pulls and spike to big move for pocket -- mantel up.

9 FACE V0
Crimp and undercling, pull over lip.

10 HAND TRAVERSE★ V3
Overhanging hand traverse using holds on the lip, from right to left.

11 THE CAVE★★★ V5
Guaranteed shade and seclusion. Start on the east end of the cave, bomb-bay chimney followed by slotting and stemming moves lead to the pull around onto a ledge and sunlight. Long and withering. The **YABO VARIATION** (harder) finishes up the face to the left using flat holds.

12 SLAB V0
Just before entering the cave, on the right. Tricky start leads to smearing, flakes and pockets.

13 FREQUENT FLYER★★★ V6
*Left side underneath boulder, SDS to top out - strenuous.

14 FIGHTING WITH ALLIGATORS★★★ V10
*Left side underneath boulder, SDS (as for 13) to outrageous traverse right - way burly.

15 RODEO STYLE★ V3
*Sidepull flake and over on positive holds - overhanging.

16 TRACK OF THE CAT★★★ V0R
An elegant climb up a long swath of perfect sandstone. Pockets will entice you to the crux; thin moves to finish. Sweet and long.

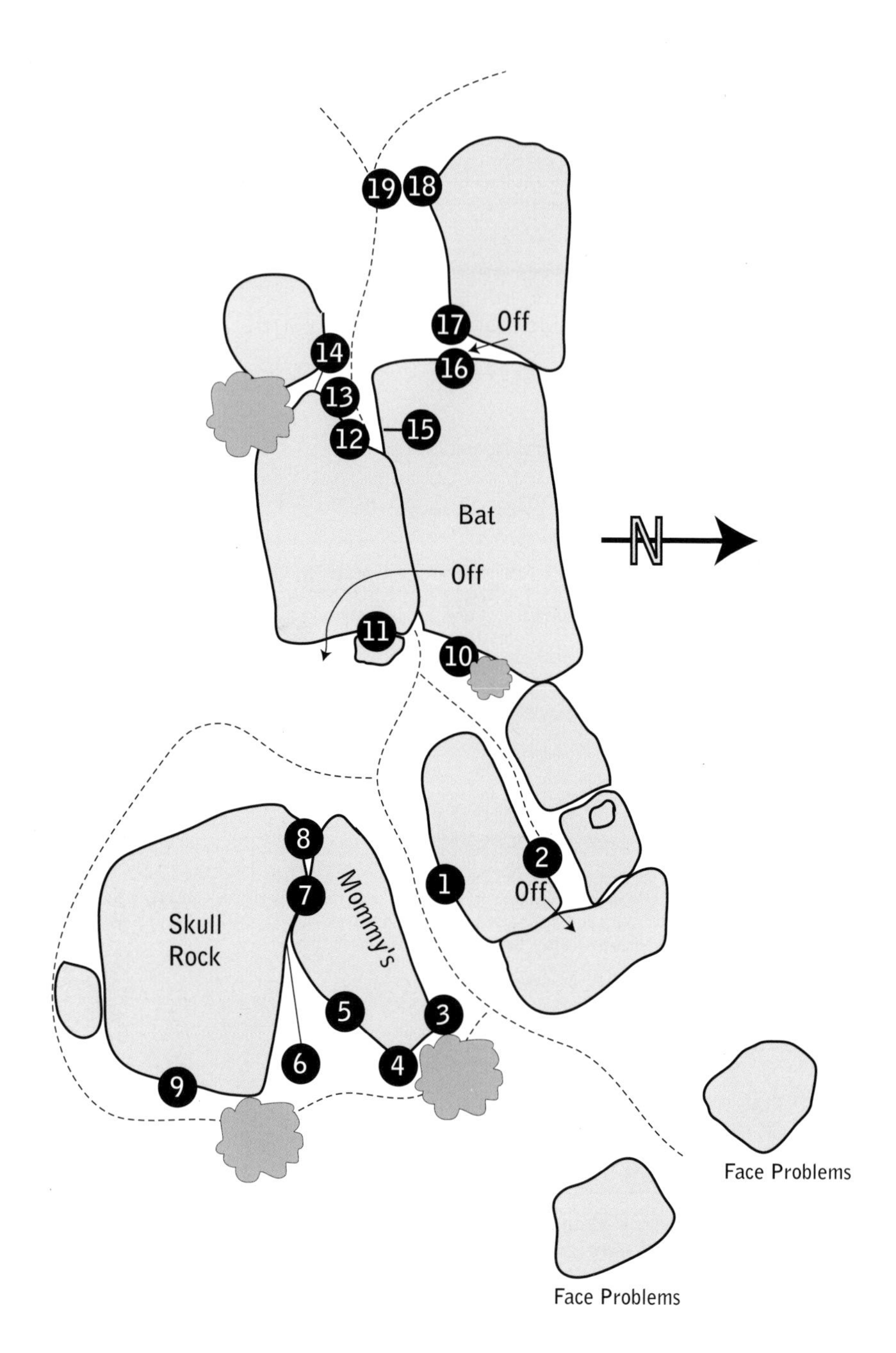

MOMMY'S BOYS AREA BOULDERS

Mommy's Boys Area Problems

nis area comprises of several large boulders in a great setting, lots of shade, great views and relative quiet. ome great problems too. What more could you want? Other routes are included on the pages that follow.

1 YABO DYNO★★ V9
Use a dyno to gain the top. A variation (**CRIMP IT OR RIP IT** V7) heads off to the right before the dyno.

2 POCKET TRAVERSE★★★ V2
Truly withering. Power moves all the way then a duet of stylish throws lead to the handrail, hand traverse then up. Up variations exist to the right and are harder.. Phew!

3 RIGHT ARETE★ V0
Pocket and edge to overhanging section.

4 LEFT ARETE V3
The left arete is harder

5 EASY FACE★ VB
The South Face of Mommy's Boys has an easy Class 5 face route.

6 SHARKS TOOTH★★ V3
This traverse starts in the fire pit and heads right using pockets to gain a move around the arete, then follow the face to end at the block below Easy Face on Skull Rock, (Route 7 on Page 117).

7 LIP MANTLE★★ VB
From Mommy's Boys pull and swing up over the lip of Skull Rock, very fun!

8 OVERHANGING FACE V0
From Route (6) up as far as possible.

9 FLAKES★ V0
This face on Skull Rock has a good little route on black patina flakes. To the right of this lies a soaring overhanging arete, one of John Yablonski's last great problems, never to be.

10 FACE★ V0
Sidepulls and technical stuff to a big pocket, and pull over onto the slab. A **VARIATION** (V1) moves further right and performs a Crowd Pleaser type move on to the ledge.

11 OFFWIDTH★ V1
Grainy stuff leads to a pocket, followed by a mantle over the lip. Remember to tape up.

12 CRY UNCLE★★★ V7
Way powerful moves lead to the undercling, shoot for the big pocket, pull over the top. Look out for tree when pulling over. Spotter required to prevent bump on opposite wall, should failure occur.

13 TWO WORLDS COLLIDE★ V9
SDS then up bald arete! Y.Kuperstein, M.Reardon.

14 TOMMY'S MY BITCH★ V8
SDS in cave then around onto slab.

15 JAM CRACK★★ VB
Jam your way out of the cave and onto the ledge. Fun.

16 LUCY★ VBR
Straight up the west face, tricky start; loose and highball. Gets your attention.

17 THIN FACE I★ V0
Crimpy, smeary moves to top. Lots of eliminates between (16) and (17) V0-V7.

18 THIN FACE II★ V0
More crimpy, smeary moves to top.

19 NILES-REARDON TRAVERSE★ V2
Crimpy traverse from (18) to finish on the hand match on (10), then head back! Mega-withering.

Mommy's Boys ~ North Face

This boulder is unusual because it lies perpendicular to the bed-plane of Stoney Point, traditional roof flakes have become face flakes, which makes it a good spot for climbing something different. Beginners should use a top-rope, there are bolt studs up on top. All of these routes are way fun.

1. LEFT ROUTE★ VB (5.4)
A tricky start leads to a lieback flake, then go right, or straight up. A little loose.

2. THE FACE★ VB (5.7)
Fun delicate moves up (sadly) chopped holds.

3. RIGHT ROUTE★★★ VB (5.8)
A "what the?" crux leads to suberb moves on positive holds.

4. MOMMY'S TRAVERSE★ V0
From left to right, thin smedging, fun and quite safe.

The Author sends(!) Right Route VB | Photo: Scott Nom

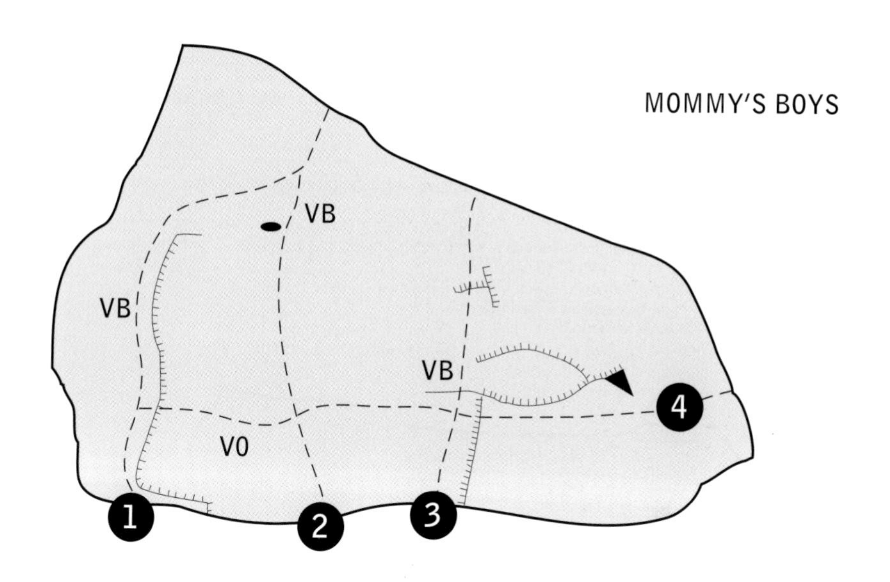

Skull Rock ~ West Side

The top can be reached by swinging over the lip as seen from the top of Mommy's Boys (7)on Page 115, highly worthwhile for its own sake), or solo up 'Easy Face'.

5 WEST FACE★ V0R
The steep face with some variations.

6 THE SKULL V1R
Up to the pockets, then strenuous moves up and right.

7 EASY FACE★ VB
A fun way to the top.

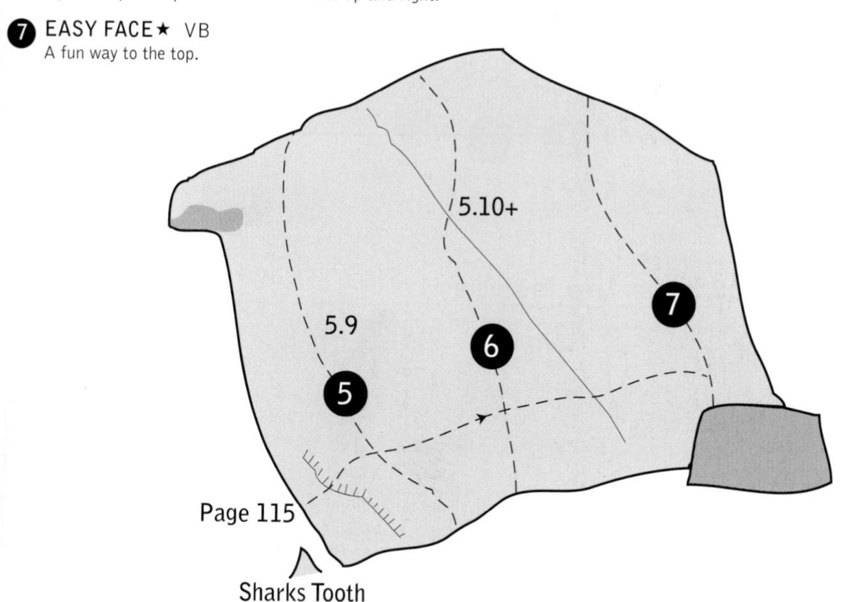

Bat Boulder ~ North Face

So called because of the red bat painted on its east face. A jump from a boulder to the south leads to the top, take slings and nuts/cams for the anchor. Route length 30′.

❶ THE BAT★ 5.9
An overhanging start; the crux, leads to moves to exit the alcove then easier climbing.

❷ NEVER SAY DIE★★ 5.10b
An even tougher overhanging start leads to steep face climbing on good holds.

❸ J.T.★ 5.8
The slab on the right by a couple of variations.

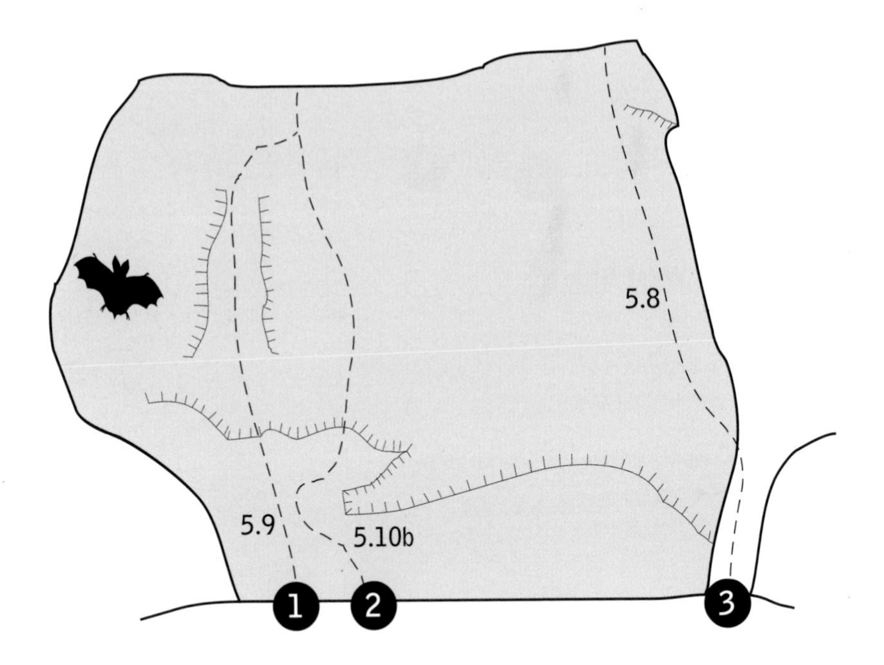

Summit Boulder Area Problems

This boulder lies just to the north of the big summit boulder (see Page 110).

❹ TRAVERSE VB
From right to left across the ledge then up the slab.

❺ UP PROBLEM V0
Pull through onto the ledge, go left then up the slab.

❻ CORN★★ V4
Deceptively hard. From left to right using the ledge as the handholds. Rock at start is off.

Tom Bristow eats Corn V4 (Page 118) | Michael Reardon Collection

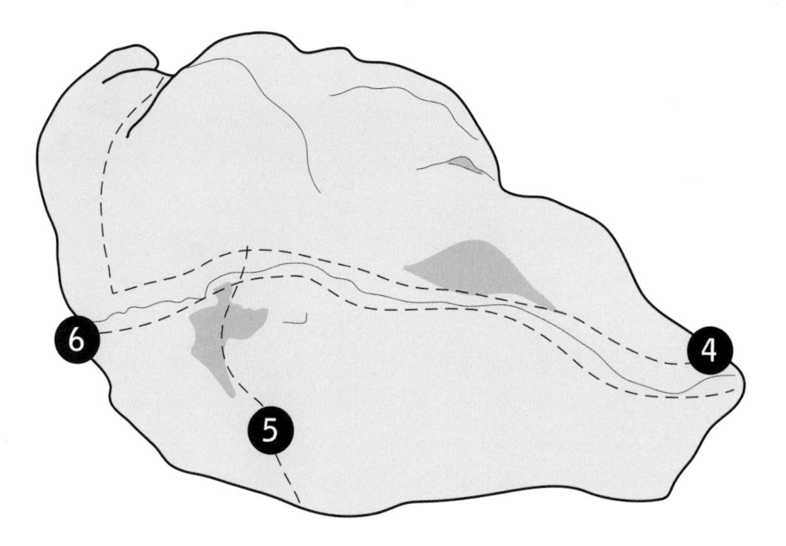

Summit Boulder

"Gentlemen, I can take you no further" - Conrad Kain on reaching the summit of Mt. Robson.

The actual summit of Stoney Point constitutes this large boulder (but how did it get here?), sadly, a popular graffiti spot, although progress is being made in this department. Two easy routes lie on this boulder and seem to be attempted more by hikers and thrill seekers than actual climbers, they are included here for completeness. Descent is via Route 1.

1 STANDARD ROUTE★ VB
Step off a boulder and up the slab, traverse right then commit over the overlap and thence to the summit.

2 LEFT VARIATION★ VB
Same start but climb up the steep section to the left to finish on the summit.

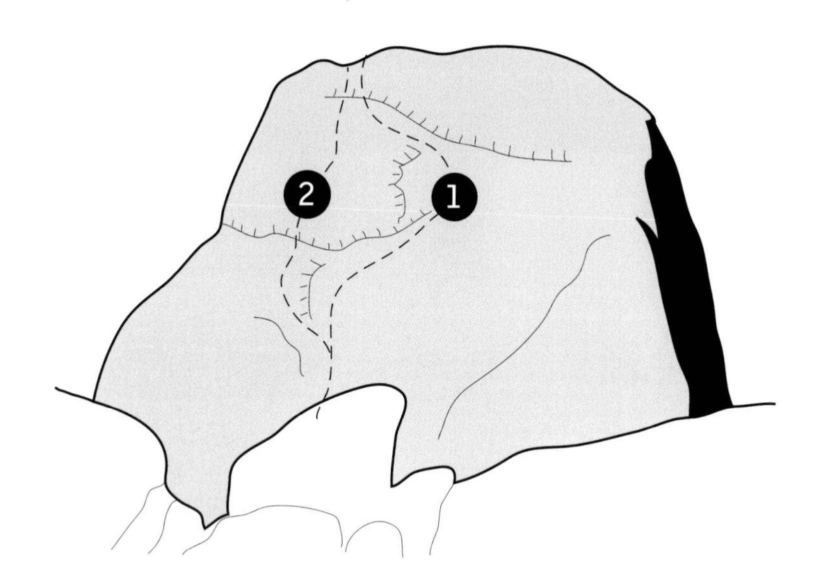

North Park Area Routes

Not much activity here and time will tell if the new addition will catch on and be developed from a bouldering point of view. It does seem like there's some potential. See map on Page 122.

1. SEAM I VB
The seam and flakes (loose) to tricky top out.

2. SEAM II★ VB
The seam with shallow pockets, cleaner than Route (1).

3. SLAB RH ROUTE★ VB
The slab on good holds.

4. TRAVERSE VB
Traverse the slab with good holds for the hands and smears for the feet.

5. SHORT ROOF★ V3
Sit start then shoot for the lip, hands up and mantle.

The following routes are top rope climbs and are located on the crag tucked in the corner of Topanga Canyon Boulevard and the 118 East on-ramp, sitting above the Old Topanga Canyon Boulevard. There seems to be more top roping potential here.

6. THE G SPOT 5.11
Up the overhanging face on large pockets, with a roof to finish.

7. THE FREEWAY CRACK★★★ 5.9
Well worth the walk, a steep lieback problem up Stoney's best looking crack. The steepness yields a little into the cave, go right and onto a ledge, then finish up a fun corner crack. Can be led.

8. CRACK I 5.8
Crack to the right of The Freeway Crack. Finish on ledge or up the fun corner of Route (7).

9. CRACK II 5.8
Another crack with a tricky start, finish on the ledge.

There's a handfull of boulders north of this crag, well seen when heading west on the 118 Freeway, looks like some potential.

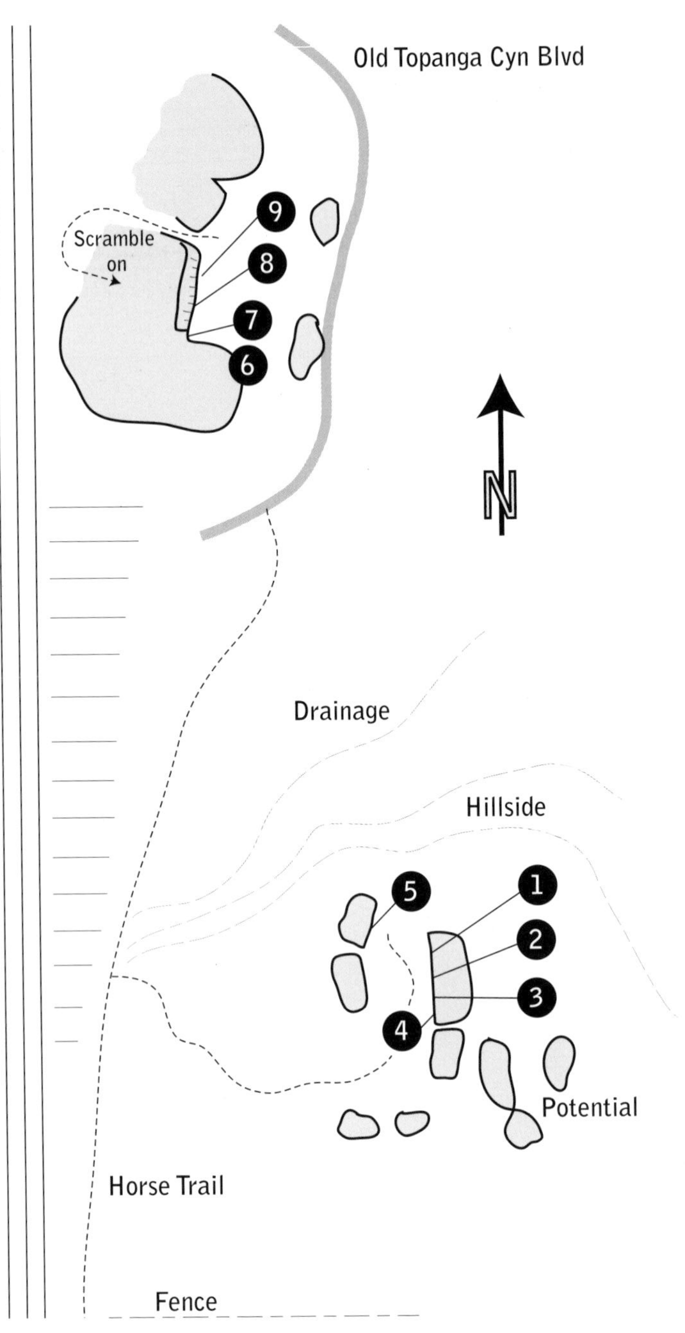

NORTH PARK AREA

bouldering circuits

VB Circuit

Tailored for beginners, these 8 problems will be sure to get your head where it needs to be, and will provide a good tour of Stoney Point and introduce the newcomer to what Stoney has to offer. Be sure to use a crash-pad or two and attentive spotters. If in doubt back off, or TR until you can head-point. Above all enjoy!

1. **WEST ARETE★★** VB
   Boulder 1 -- See Page 14.
2. **THE JAM CRACK★★** VB
   Jam Rock -- See Page 16.
3. **QUOTATION MARKS★** VB
   Pile Ups -- See Page 35.
4. **UNTOLD STORY★★★** VB
   Turlock -- See Page 46.
5. **THE CHIMNEY★★** VB
   Split Rock -- See Page 62.
6. **SW CORNER★★★** V0
   Carousel Rock -- See Page 94
7. **RIGHT ROUTE★★★** VB (5.8)
   Mommys Boys -- See Page 116
8. **LEFT ROUTE★** VB (5.4)
   Mommys Boys -- See Page 116

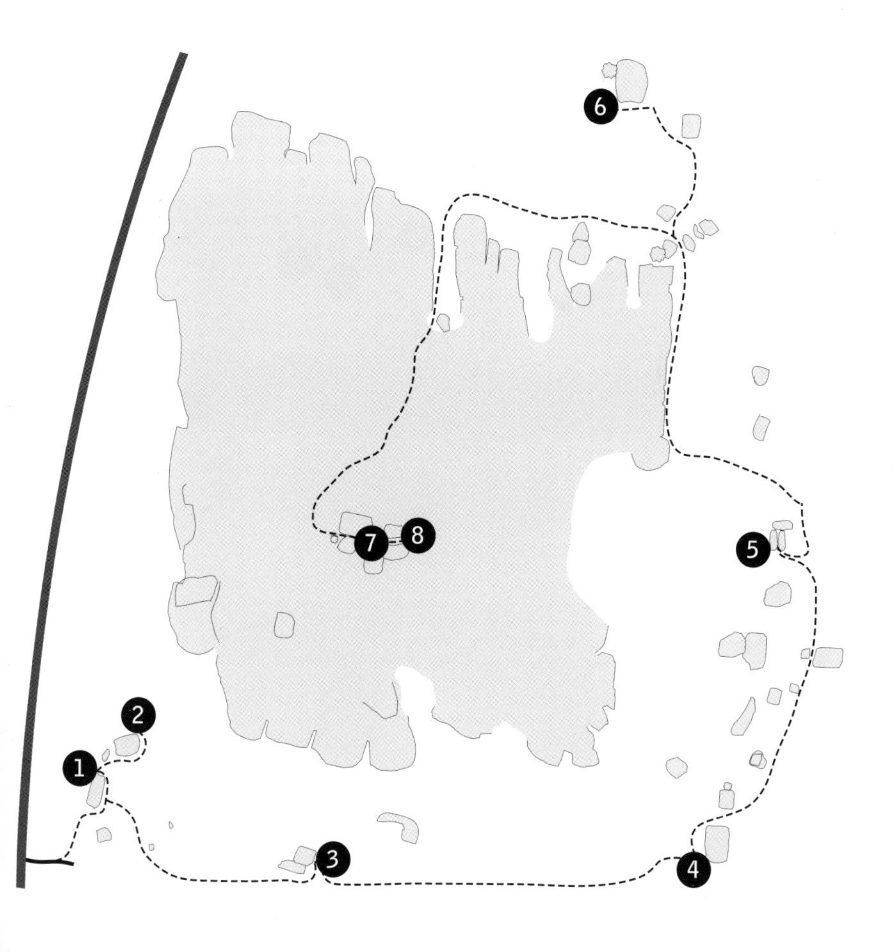

SoWR Circuit

I don't claim for one minute to have enchained these traverses first, rather, I include this circuit here as a tribute to all of those Wednesday evenings that I've spend with my friends, solving the World's problems while moving sideways. Once these traverses feel easy, it's time to head back in the opposite direction.

1. **TODD'S TRAVERSE★★★** V0
   Amphitheater -- See Page 36.
2. **SPIRAL TRAVERSE★★★** V1
   Spiral Boulder -- See Page 61.
3. **POTHOLES TRAVERSE★★★** V1
   The Back Wall -- See Page 69.
4. **MOZART'S TRAVERSE★★★** V0
   Mozart's Wall -- See Page 80.
5. **SCULPTURE'S TRAVERSE★★★** V3
   Sculpture's Crack Wall -- See Page 82.
6. **NABISCO TRAVERSE★★★** V1
   Nabisco Canyon -- See Page 84.

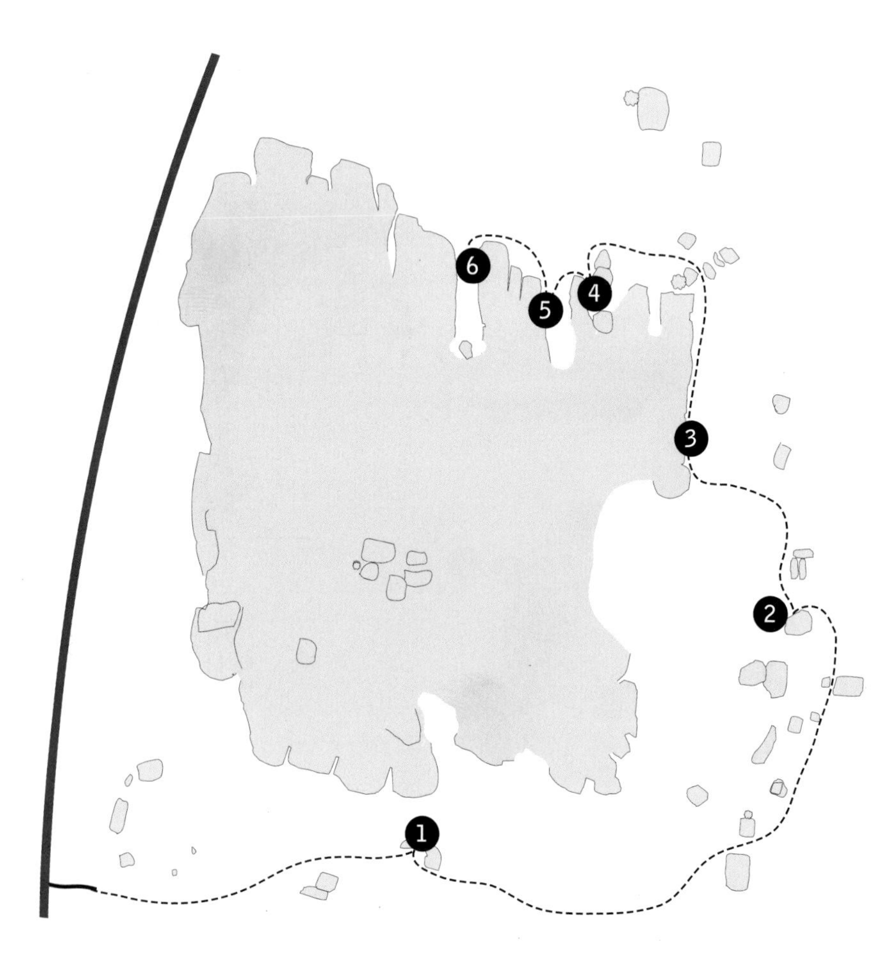

routes by rating

Top Rope Routes

5.0 - 5.6

- ❑ ARCH CHIMNEY 5.5 24
- ❑ BEEHIVE★★★ 5.4 69
- ❑ CHIMNEY, THE 5.5 42
- ❑ MAIN CHIMNEY, THE★ 5.6 105
- ❑ RIGHT EDGE★★ 5.5 80
- ❑ S-CRACK★★★ 5.4 105
- ❑ SCARFACE★ 5.6 41
- ❑ SPENCER'S SLAB LEFT★★ 5.5 31

5.7

- ❑ BEETHOVEN'S CRACK★★ 5.7 79
- ❑ BLACK'S CRACK★★ 5.7 69
- ❑ CHATSWORTH CHIMNEY 5.7 23
- ❑ CHIMNEY 5.7 69
- ❑ CHIMNEY★ 5.7 84
- ❑ CROWN OF THORNS★★ 5.7 24
- ❑ EAST WALL GROOVE★ 5.7 84
- ❑ FLAKY CRACK★ 5.7 22
- ❑ FROSTED FLAKES★★★ 5.7 103
- ❑ LEFTHAND ROUTE★★★ 5.7 80
- ❑ MANTLE START★★ 5.7 79
- ❑ NABISCO★★ 5.7 84
- ❑ OVERHANG PASSBY★ 5.7 55
- ❑ POTHOLES ESCAPE★★ 5.7 69

5.8

- ❑ CRACK I 5.8 121
- ❑ CRACK II 5.8 121
- ❑ CRACK, THE 5.8 107
- ❑ CRACK, THE 5.8R 23
- ❑ FAR LEFT ROUTE80 5.8 ★
- ❑ J.T.118 5.8 ★
- ❑ LEFT CRACK89 5.8 ★
- ❑ LEFTHAND CRACK102 5.8 ★
- ❑ PEDESTAL CRACK102 5.8 ★
- ❑ RH ROUTE84 5.8 ★★
- ❑ RIDDLER, THE27 5.8 ★★
- ❑ RIGHT-HAND CRACK 5.8 22
- ❑ SLAB ROUTE 5.8 22
- ❑ STUDLEY SLAB 5.8 24

5.9

- ❑ A-FRAME RIGHT69 5.9 ★★★
- ❑ BAT, THE118 5.9 ★
- ❑ BLACK CRACK32 5.9 ★
- ❑ BRACKET, THE21 5.9 ★
- ❑ CENTER ROUTE80 5.9 ★★★
- ❑ CONNECTIONS29 5.9 ★
- ❑ EAST WALL ELIMINATE84 5.9 ★
- ❑ EASY MONEY 5.9 56
- ❑ FLAKESTORM89 5.9+ ★★
- ❑ FLYING FISH88 5.9 ★
- ❑ FREEWAY CRACK, THE121 5.9 ★★★
- ❑ FRONT ROUTE 5.9 31
- ❑ HEART OF GLASS86 5.9 ★
- ❑ JOHNNY CAT40 5.9+ ★
- ❑ LEFT EDGE86 5.9 ★
- ❑ LEFT ROUTE 5.9+ 39
- ❑ LEFT ROUTE84 5.9 ★
- ❑ LITTLE JESUS107 5.9 ★
- ❑ MAGNUM CASE41 5.9 ★
- ❑ NOW VOYAGER 5.9 29
- ❑ O-ZONE, THE88 5.9+ ★★
- ❑ PAUL'S HOLE29 5.9 ★★★

5.9 continued

- ❑ PILLAR LEFT★ 5.9 23
- ❑ PIN SCARS★★★ 5.9 41
- ❑ PINK DRIPS★★★ 5.9 21
- ❑ POTHOLES CRACK★ 5.9 69
- ❑ POTHOLES★★ 5.9 69
- ❑ QUICKSILVER 5.9+ 83
- ❑ RED DAWN★ 5.9+ 50
- ❑ RIGHT EDGE★ 5.9 86
- ❑ RIGHT ROUTE★ 5.9+ 39
- ❑ RIGHT-HAND ROUTE★ 5.9 21
- ❑ SANDSTORM★ 5.9 89
- ❑ TIERDROP★ 5.9 22
- ❑ VARIATION I★ 5.9 107
- ❑ WALL AND SLAB 5.9 83

5.10

- ❑ 5.9 SLAB, THE★ 5.10c 96
- ❑ 747★★★ 5.10c 86
- ❑ A PCKTFUL OF TENDONITIS★ 5.10c 86
- ❑ A-FRAME LEFT 5.10b 69
- ❑ AMADEUS II★★ 5.10a 80
- ❑ AMADEUS★★ 5.10a 80
- ❑ BOLTED LEAD 5.10aR 27
- ❑ BULL MARKET★ 5.10c 56
- ❑ CENTER ROUTE★★ 5.10a 79
- ❑ CHANGELING★★ 5.10d 42
- ❑ CHOCKSTONE WALL 5.10a 28
- ❑ COSMIC CORNER 5.10d 86
- ❑ CRUCIFIX★★ 5.10b/c 107
- ❑ DEAD CENTER★ 5.10a 80
- ❑ DIRECT ROUTE★ 5.10c 79
- ❑ DIRECT★★ 5.10b/c 21
- ❑ EAT OR BE EATEN★★★ 5.10c 88
- ❑ EYE OF FAITH★★★ 5.10c 29
- ❑ HOLY S^^T★ 5.10d 96
- ❑ JESUS WALL LEFT★★★ 5.10c 107
- ❑ JESUS WALL★★★ 5.10c 107
- ❑ KILLER BEES★ 5.10+ 105
- ❑ LEFT ARETE★ 5.10a 21
- ❑ LEFT EDGE★★ 5.10b 107
- ❑ MANTLEPEACE★ 5.10c 23
- ❑ MERCURY 5.10a 83
- ❑ MUGNESEA LUNG★★ 5.10a 28
- ❑ NEVER SAY DIE★★ 5.10b 118
- ❑ NORTHWEST PASSAGE★ 5.10+ 102
- ❑ NUTCRACKER★★★ 5.10a 86
- ❑ OFFSET SLAB★ 5.10a 31
- ❑ OVERLORD★ 5.10b 55
- ❑ OWL HOLE★ 5.10c 69
- ❑ PILLAR RIGHT★ 5.10a 23
- ❑ POCKET ROCKET★ 5.10a 24
- ❑ PREYING MANTIS★ 5.10b 65
- ❑ RABBIT'S FOOT★ 5.10c 55
- ❑ RAINBOW'S END★★ 5.10+ 24
- ❑ ROUTE RUSTLIN'★ 5.10+ 98
- ❑ SAVAGE SLAB★★ 5.10a 28
- ❑ SCULPTED CRACK L★★ 5.10c 82
- ❑ SCULPTURE'S CRACK★★★ 5.10c 82
- ❑ SHARK'S TOOTH, THE 5.10b/c 89
- ❑ SPENCER'S SLAB RIGHT★ 5.10a 31
- ❑ STORMWARNING★ 5.10c 89
- ❑ SWEET SUBURBIA★★ 5.10+ 103
- ❑ TELEPHONE BOOTH 5.10b 69
- ❑ TIDY CAT★ 5.10a 40
- ❑ TONY THE TIGER★★ 5.10+ 103
- ❑ UNDERWORLD★★ 5.10b 21
- ❑ VARIATION I★ 5.10a 88
- ❑ VARIATION II★ 5.10+ 107
- ❑ VARIATION II★ 5.10+ 88
- ❑ WINGED MESSENGER★ 5.10b 83
- ❑ WOUNDED KNEE★★ 5.10d 21
- ❑ WRATH OF KAHAN, THE★ 5.10d 69
- ❑ YARD THE TOOL★ 5.10a/b 98

5.11

- ❑ 5.10 SLAB, THE 5.11a 96
- ❑ BATMAN AND OWEN★ 5.11a 27
- ❑ BEEGONE★ 5.11a 69
- ❑ BLACK FRIDAY★ 5.11b 56
- ❑ BLACK MONDAY★ 5.11+ 56
- ❑ BLACK WALL, THE★★★ 5.11a 32
- ❑ CAPTAIN ENERGY★ 5.11a 65
- ❑ CARLSBURG★ 5.11b 82
- ❑ CENTRAL ROUTE★★★ 5.11a 107
- ❑ CIRCUS GAMES★ 5.11 103
- ❑ COLD TURKEY★ 5.11b/c 88
- ❑ G SPOT, THE 5.11 121
- ❑ IGUANA★★ 5.11c 84
- ❑ KAIRO★ 5.11a 102
- ❑ LAND SHARK 5.11b/c 89
- ❑ LAYED OFF★ 5.11a 55
- ❑ LEFT EDGE★★ 5.11+ 79
- ❑ MAGGIE'S FARM★★★ 5.11b 84
- ❑ MANTIS MANTLE 5.11a 65
- ❑ MIDDLE ROUTE 5.11- 55
- ❑ NUTCRACKER DIRECT★★ 5.11c 86
- ❑ OZYMANDIAS★★★ 5.11b 105
- ❑ PICK POCKET★ 5.11b 105
- ❑ PROW, THE★★★ 5.11a 79
- ❑ RIGHT ROUTE 5.11+ 30
- ❑ SAND BLAST★ 5.11c 82
- ❑ SCULPTED CRACK R★★ 5.11b 82
- ❑ SEMIDETACHED★★ 5.11+ 30
- ❑ VARIATION FINISH 5.11 105
- ❑ VARIATION FINISH★ 5.11a 88
- ❑ VAR START TO THE PROW★★ 5.11a 79

5.12

- ❑ DART LADY 5.12 69
- ❑ DYNOMITE★ 5.12 79
- ❑ I HAVE FAITH★★ 5.12 105
- ❑ MAIN WALL★★ 5.12 105
- ❑ SCURF★★ 5.12 84
- ❑ THE PLANK 5.12 69
- ❑ VICIOUS★★ 5.12 69

5.13

- ❑ SPROUT WINGS & FLY★ 5.13? 84

Aid

- ❑ BOLT LADDER 5.6, C1 107

Boulder Problems

(YDS in parenthesis indicates that route may also be traditionally top-roped.)

VB

- ❑ ACE'S TRAVERSE★ VB 70
- ❑ ARETE VB 76
- ❑ ARETE★ VB 74
- ❑ BEGINNER'S SLAB VB 58
- ❑ CAROUSEL EDGE★ VB 94
- ❑ CAROUSEL FACE★ VB 94
- ❑ CHIMNEY, THE★★ VB 62
- ❑ CHOUINARD'S SLAB★ VB 61
- ❑ COMPOSURE★★★ VB (5.9) 58
- ❑ CRACK VB 99
- ❑ EAST FACE ROUTE VB 14
- ❑ EASY FACE VB 74
- ❑ EASY FACE★ VB 117
- ❑ EASY FACE★★ VB 74
- ❑ EASY MONEY VB (5.9) 56
- ❑ EDGE, THE VB 13
- ❑ FACE VB 74
- ❑ FACE & SLAB I★ VB 113
- ❑ FACE★ VB 16, 74
- ❑ FACE, THE★ VB (5.7) 116
- ❑ FLAKE, THE★★★ VB (5.7) 45
- ❑ JAM CRACK★★ VB 115
- ❑ JAM CRACK, THE★★ VB 16
- ❑ LEFT ROUTE★ VB (5.4) 116
- ❑ LEFT SLAB ROUTE★ VB (5.6) 58
- ❑ LEFT VARIATION★ VB 120
- ❑ LIEBACK FLAKE★★ VB 58
- ❑ LIP MANTLE★★ VB 115
- ❑ LUCY★ VBR 115
- ❑ MR TOAD'S WILD RIDE★★ VB (5.8+) 81
- ❑ NORTH FACE★ VB (5.7) 46
- ❑ NORTH FLAKE★★★ VB (5.7) 46
- ❑ NORTH SIDE LH VB 13
- ❑ NOSE, THE★★★ VB 15
- ❑ POTHOLES★ VB (5.6) 46
- ❑ QUOTATION MARKS★ VB 35
- ❑ RIGHT ROUTE★★★ VB (5.8) 116
- ❑ ROOF & MANTLE VB 35
- ❑ SEAM I VB 121
- ❑ SEAM II★ VB 121
- ❑ SHORT STORY★★ VB 14
- ❑ SLAB RH ROUTE★ VB 121
- ❑ SLAB★ VBR 36
- ❑ SLAB, THE VB 13
- ❑ SLAB, THE★★ VB (5.6) 58
- ❑ SLIDE, THE★ VB (5.8) 58
- ❑ STAIRS, THE★ VB 45
- ❑ STANDARD ROUTE★ VB 120
- ❑ TEXAS FLAKE FACE★ VB 84
- ❑ TRAVERSE VB 118, 121
- ❑ UNTOLD STORY★★★ VB 46
- ❑ VENGABOYS★ VB 99
- ❑ VIVARIN VB14 ★
- ❑ WE LIKE TO PARTY★ VB 99
- ❑ WEST ARETE★★ VB 14
- ❑ WEST FACE★ VB 16

V0

- ❑ ANT LINE★★ V0 58
- ❑ ARETE V0 76
- ❑ ARETE★ V0 13, 76, 81
- ❑ ARETE SKELETON V0 (5.10c) 62
- ❑ ARETE WITH NO NAME★ V0 74
- ❑ BEETHOVEN'S TRAVERSE★ V0 79
- ❑ BLACK ROOF, THE★ V0R 36
- ❑ BOLDDURING★ V0R (5.10a) 61
- ❑ BONEHOLE★ V0 100
- ❑ BOREALIS★ V0R (5.9+) 61
- ❑ BULGE V0 99
- ❑ BULGE★ V0 66
- ❑ BULL MARKET★ V0 (5.10c) 56
- ❑ CORNER, THE★★ V0 48
- ❑ CRACK V0 74, 94
- ❑ CRACK HAND-TRAVERSE★ V0R 90
- ❑ CRACK★ V0 79
- ❑ CRITTER CRACK★★★ V0 74

V0 continued

- ❑ CROWD TEASER V0 46
- ❑ DIHEDRAL LEFT V0 15
- ❑ DIHEDRAL RIGHT V0 15
- ❑ DON'T GIVE ME NO LIP★ V0 99
- ❑ EARTHQUAKE PROBLEM★★ V0R 76
- ❑ EAST FACE★ V0 35
- ❑ FACE V0 16, 57, 81, 113
- ❑ FACE & SLAB II★ V0 113
- ❑ FACE ELIMINATE★ V0 46
- ❑ FACE OPPOSITE PYRAMID★ V0 57
- ❑ FACE V0 70
- ❑ FACE★ V0 18, 50, 94, 111, 115
- ❑ FACE★★ V0 54, 74
- ❑ IGUANA TRAVERSE★ V0 84
- ❑ JAM CRACK★ V0 69
- ❑ LEFT FACE V0 18
- ❑ MANTLES V0 13, 113
- ❑ MEAT GRINDER MANTLE★ VB 58
- ❑ MIKE'S UP PROBLEM V0 36
- ❑ MOMMY'S TRAVERSE★ V0 116
- ❑ MOZART'S TRAVERSE★★★ V0 80
- ❑ NORTH FACE MANTLE★ V0 16
- ❑ NORTH SIDE R★★★ V0 13
- ❑ NOSE ELIMINATE★★ V0 15
- ❑ ORIGINAL START★ V0 76
- ❑ OVERHANGING FACE V0 115
- ❑ PIE SLICE V0 58
- ❑ PIN SCARS (SILENT RUNNING)★ V0 45
- ❑ RAMADA★★ V0R 46
- ❑ RAMP V0 76
- ❑ RIGHT ARETE★ V0 115
- ❑ ROOF & ARETE V0 90
- ❑ SANCTUARY V0 94
- ❑ SHORTY SHEA V0R 74
- ❑ SLAB V0 113
- ❑ SLAB II★★ V0 57
- ❑ SLAB★ V0 94, 99
- ❑ SMEDGE★★ V0 (5.10a) 58
- ❑ SOUTH FACE V0R 16
- ❑ SPIRAL DIRECT II V0 61
- ❑ SPIRAL DIRECT★ V0 61
- ❑ SW CORNER★★★ V0 94
- ❑ THIN FACE I★ V0 115
- ❑ THIN FACE II★ V0 115
- ❑ THIN FACE V0 70
- ❑ THREE PIGS★ V0 15
- ❑ TODD'S TRAVERSE★★★ V0 36
- ❑ TRACK OF THE CAT★★★ V0R 113
- ❑ TROUBLE TOLD★★ V0 96
- ❑ TURLOCK ELIMINATE★ V0 45
- ❑ TURLOCK FACE★ V0 45
- ❑ UMMAGUMMA CRACK★ V0 111
- ❑ UP PROBLEM V0 118
- ❑ VARIATION V0 94
- ❑ WEST FACE★ V0R 117

V1

- ❑ 10-40 V1 15
- ❑ ALICE IN SLANDERLAND★★ V1 98
- ❑ ARETE LEFT★ V1 18
- ❑ ARETE RIGHT★ V1 18
- ❑ ARETE★ V1 94
- ❑ BIRD HOLE, THE★ V1 74
- ❑ BODY GERMAN★ V1 57
- ❑ BULGE V1 57
- ❑ BULGE, THE★ V1 45
- ❑ CORNER THE MARKET★★ V1 (5.11a) 56
- ❑ CORRIDOR TRAVERSE★ V1 76
- ❑ DARK SIDE OF THE RAINBOW V1 64
- ❑ EAST FACE V1 - V3 57
- ❑ HAND CRACK V1 81
- ❑ HOG TIED★★ V1R 48
- ❑ HOOF AND MOUTH★★★ V1 46
- ❑ LIP TRAVERSE★★ V1 35
- ❑ MAGGIE'S TRAVERSE★★★ V1 84
- ❑ MANTLE PROBLEM★★ V1 54
- ❑ MANTLELOBOTOMY★ V1 74
- ❑ NUTCRACKER CYN TRAVERSE★ V1 86
- ❑ NYLON BOY★ V1 14

V1 continued

- ❑ OFFWIDTH★ V1 115
- ❑ OZONE FACTOR V1 74
- ❑ PACKER CRACKER V1 39
- ❑ PLIERS★★ V1 46
- ❑ POTHOLES TRAVERSE★★★ V1 69
- ❑ PUMP ARETE★ V1 16
- ❑ PUMP TRAVERSE, THE★★★ V1 16
- ❑ REGGAE ROUTE★★ V1 (5.10+) 96
- ❑ RIGHT ARETE★ V1 16
- ❑ ROCK AROUND THE CLOCK★★ V1 45
- ❑ SLAB I★ V1 57
- ❑ SLANDERLAND V1 96
- ❑ SLAP★ V1 61
- ❑ SLIME★★ V1 46
- ❑ SPIRAL TRAVERSE★★★ V1 61
- ❑ SPLIT DECISION★★★ V1R 62
- ❑ SPOOKY★★ V1R 74
- ❑ STICKY FINGERS★ V1 113
- ❑ SUGAR POPS V1 58
- ❑ SKULL, THE V1R 117
- ❑ TRUE MANTLE★ V1 16
- ❑ TWO SCOOPS★ V1 48
- ❑ UNDERCLING V1 15
- ❑ UNDERCLING TRAVERSE V1 90
- ❑ VALDEZ★ V1 62
- ❑ VARIATION V1 115
- ❑ VARIATION START II V1 94
- ❑ VARIATION START★★ V1 94

V2

- ❑ ARETE V2 16
- ❑ ARETE DIRECT★ V2 18
- ❑ BLACK AND BLUE V2 64
- ❑ BLACK FRIDAY★ V2 (5.11)b 56
- ❑ BOOT FLAKE★★★ V2 14
- ❑ BUSH DOCTOR V2 100
- ❑ CAVE★ V2R 94
- ❑ CHOUINARD'S HOLE★★★ V2 100
- ❑ CORNER, THE★ V2 45
- ❑ CROWD PLEASER★★★ V2R 46
- ❑ FACE V2 54
- ❑ FACE V2R 35
- ❑ FACE★ V2 54, 94
- ❑ FLAKE TO NOWHERE★★ V2 74
- ❑ LEFT OF ARETE V2 94
- ❑ LIP TRAVERSE★ V2 113
- ❑ NILES-REARDON TRAVERSE★ V2 115
- ❑ PANCAKE★★ V2 74
- ❑ PILE LIEBACK★★★ V2 35
- ❑ POCKET TRAVERSE★★★ V2 115
- ❑ QUICKSTEP★★★ V2 81
- ❑ RIGHT ARETE V2 76
- ❑ ROLLERCOASTER, THE★★ V2R 94
- ❑ SE CORNER★ V2 15
- ❑ SEAM V2R 90
- ❑ SPIRAL LOW TRAVERSE★★★ V2 61
- ❑ STANDARD ROUTE★★ V2 62
- ❑ TEXAS FLAKE OVERHANG★★ V2R 84

V3

- ❑ BLACK MONDAY★ V3 (5.11+) 56
- ❑ BLACK ROOF, THE - LEFT SIDE V3R 36
- ❑ CLEARED FOR TAKEOFF★ V3R 93
- ❑ CRACK, THE★★★ V3 48
- ❑ DYNAMIC DUO V3 62
- ❑ EAST FACE V1 - V3 57
- ❑ EAT OUT MORE OFTEN★★ V3 62
- ❑ ENDO BOY★★ V3 14
- ❑ FACE★ V3 54, 113
- ❑ HAND TRAVERSE★ V3 113
- ❑ HEIN FLAKE V3 111
- ❑ KODIAK CORNER V3 74
- ❑ LEFT ARETE V3 115
- ❑ LOW TRAVERSE★★ V3 36
- ❑ PILEDRIVER★★★ V3 35
- ❑ PIN SCARS★ V3 36

V3 continued

V4

V5

V6

V7

V8

V9

V10

index

Symbols

A

B

C

D

E

F

G

H

I

J

K

L

M

N

S

T

U

V

W

Y

WWW.DMMWALES.COM

SAFE, SOLID, SECURE

Belay Master 2 - Safety comes first

Belay Master 2

Belay carabiners don't always behave as you might want them to. There is potential for the biner to flip into a bad alignment and for cross loading to occur.

All carabiners are designed to be strongest when loaded lengthways, so a biner loaded across ways is much weaker. With this in mind we came up with a special clip that once locked in position prevents cross loading occurring by holding the biner and belay device in the correct alignment.

There is another advantage too: the clip can only be locked if the Screwgate has been properly closed first.

We've given it a Taper Lock nose with a flared profile on the nose of the biner which significantly increases the side loading strength of the gate. The Belay Master 2 is also surprisingly light.

So there it is, one of the safest belay biners ever made which has proved very popular with climbing walls and outdoor centres.

FEATURES

- Super safe belay biner
- Plastic clip prevents cross-loading
- Taper lock nose for greater gate strength in all directions
- Strong and light I-Beam construction
- Available with Screwgate locking system